FLOWER GIRL COLORING BOOK

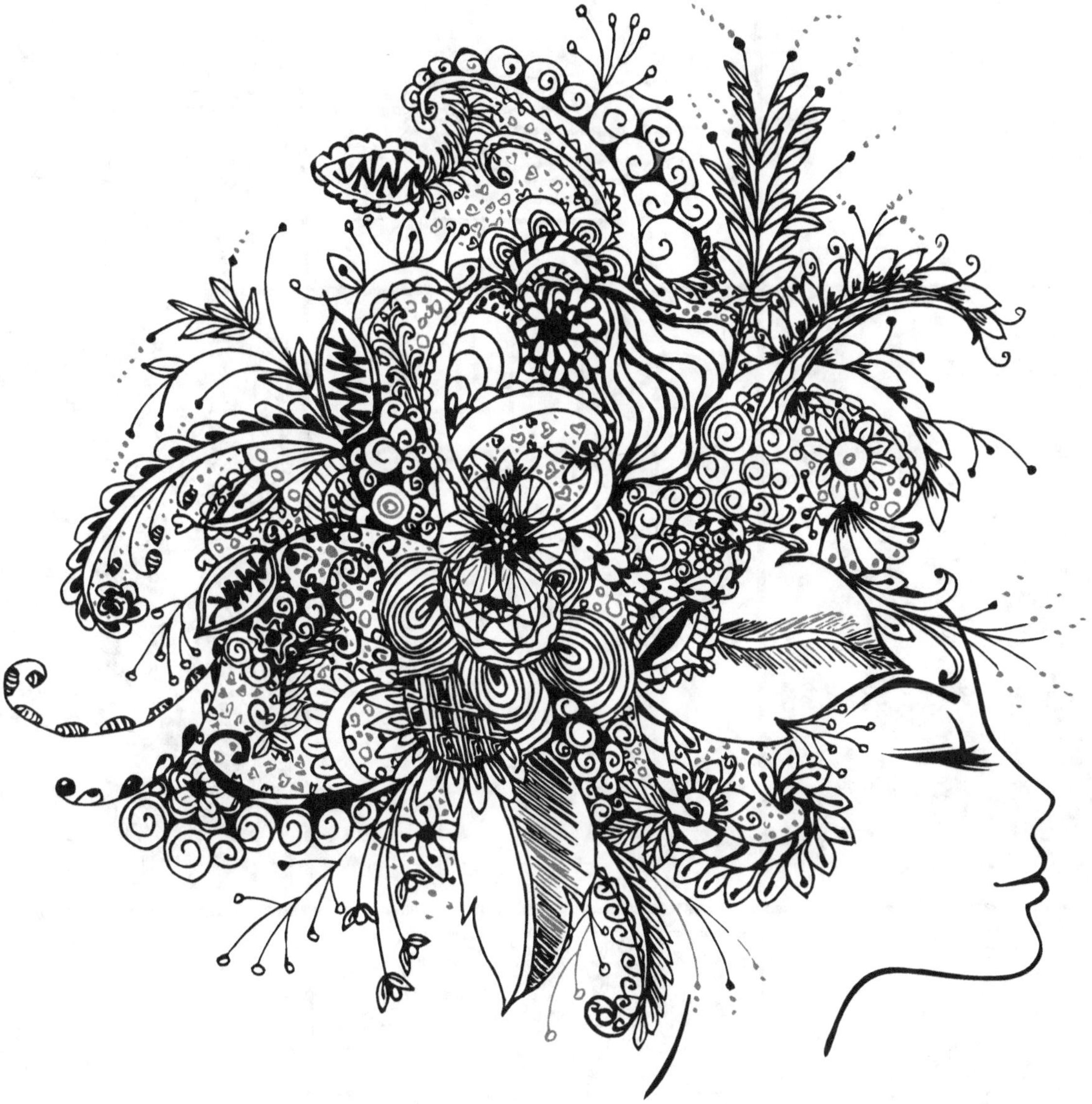

— RUSS FOCUS —

ISBN-13: 978-1727268881   ISBN-10: 1727268881

PUBLISHED BY RUSS FOCUS COPYRIGHT © 2018 ALL RIGHTS RESERVED
NO PART OF THIS PUBLICATION MAY BE REPRODUCED IN ANY
FORM OR BY ANY MEANS WITHOUT WRITTEN PERMISSION OF THE PUBLISHER.
WE ARE NOT RESPONSIBLE FOR UNSOLICITES MATERIAL PUBLISHED IN USA

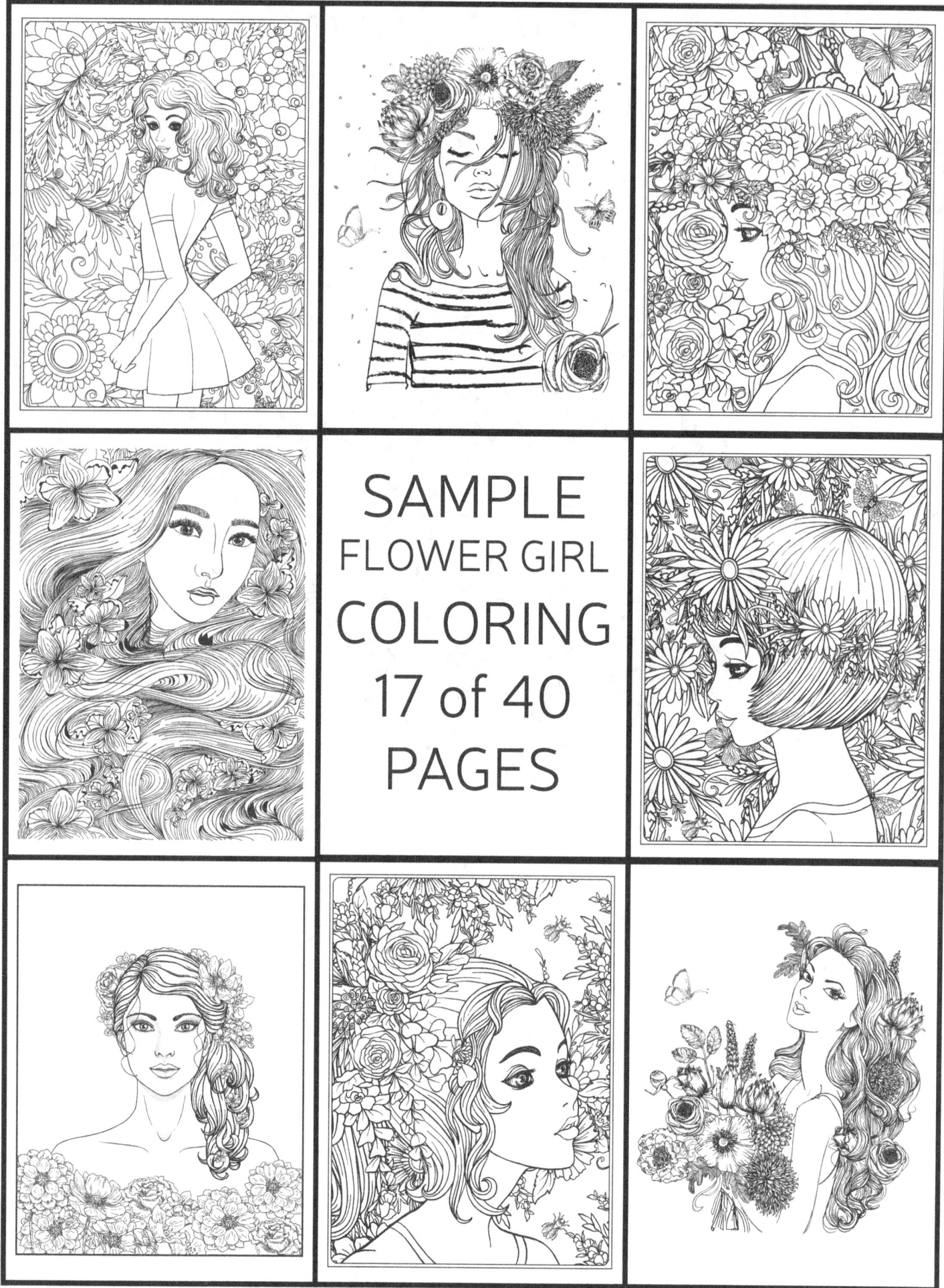

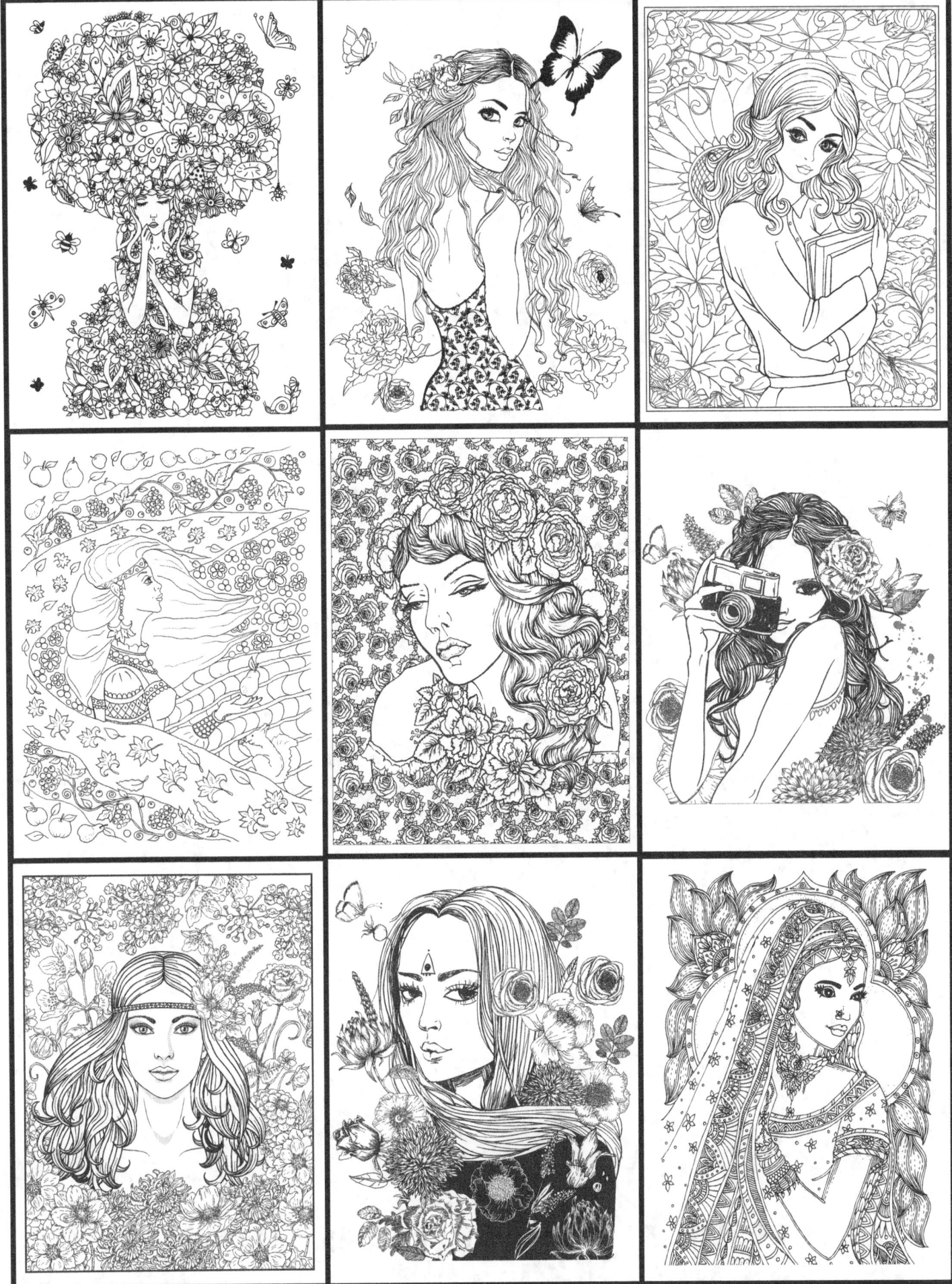

www.russfocus.com

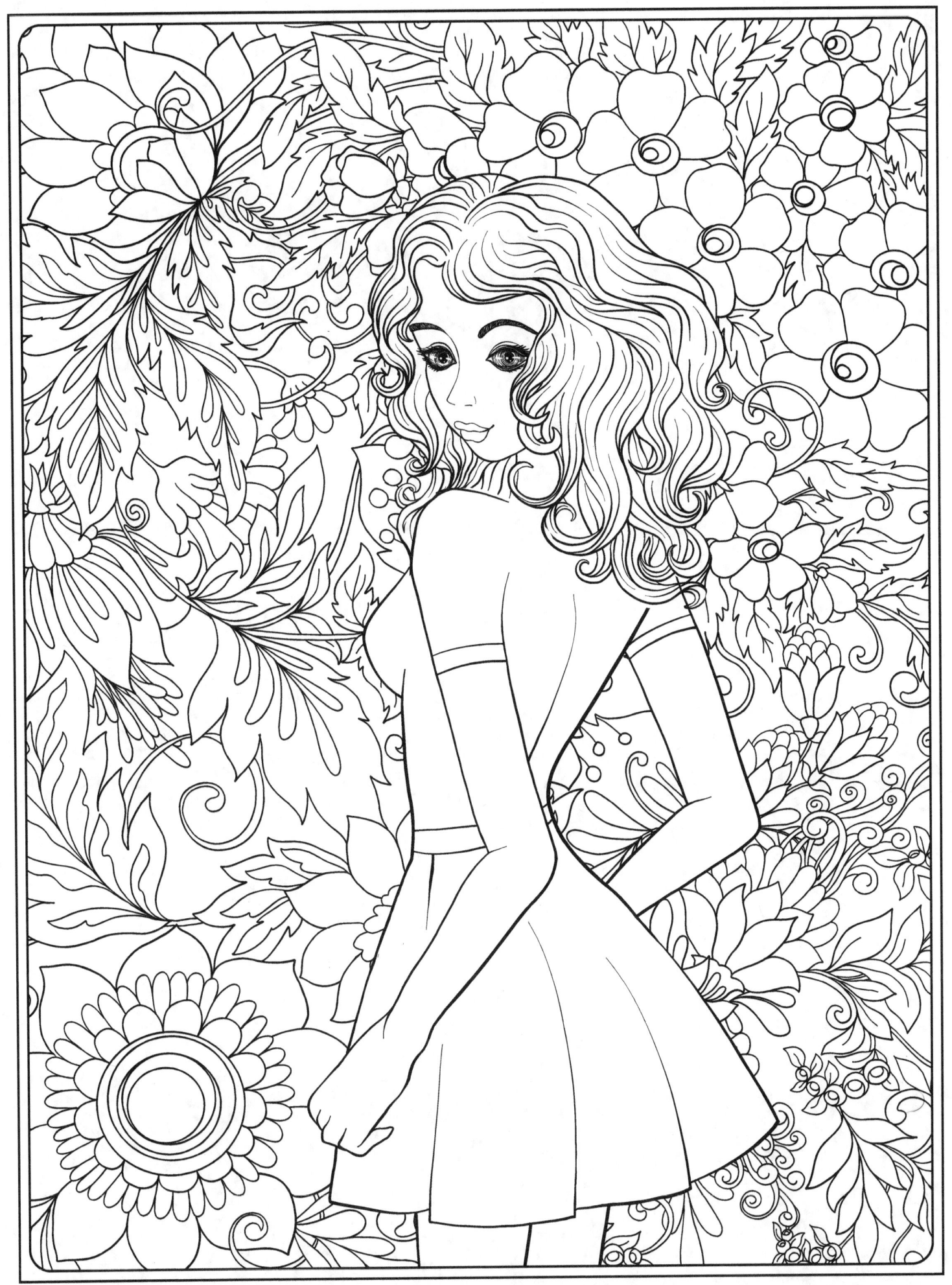

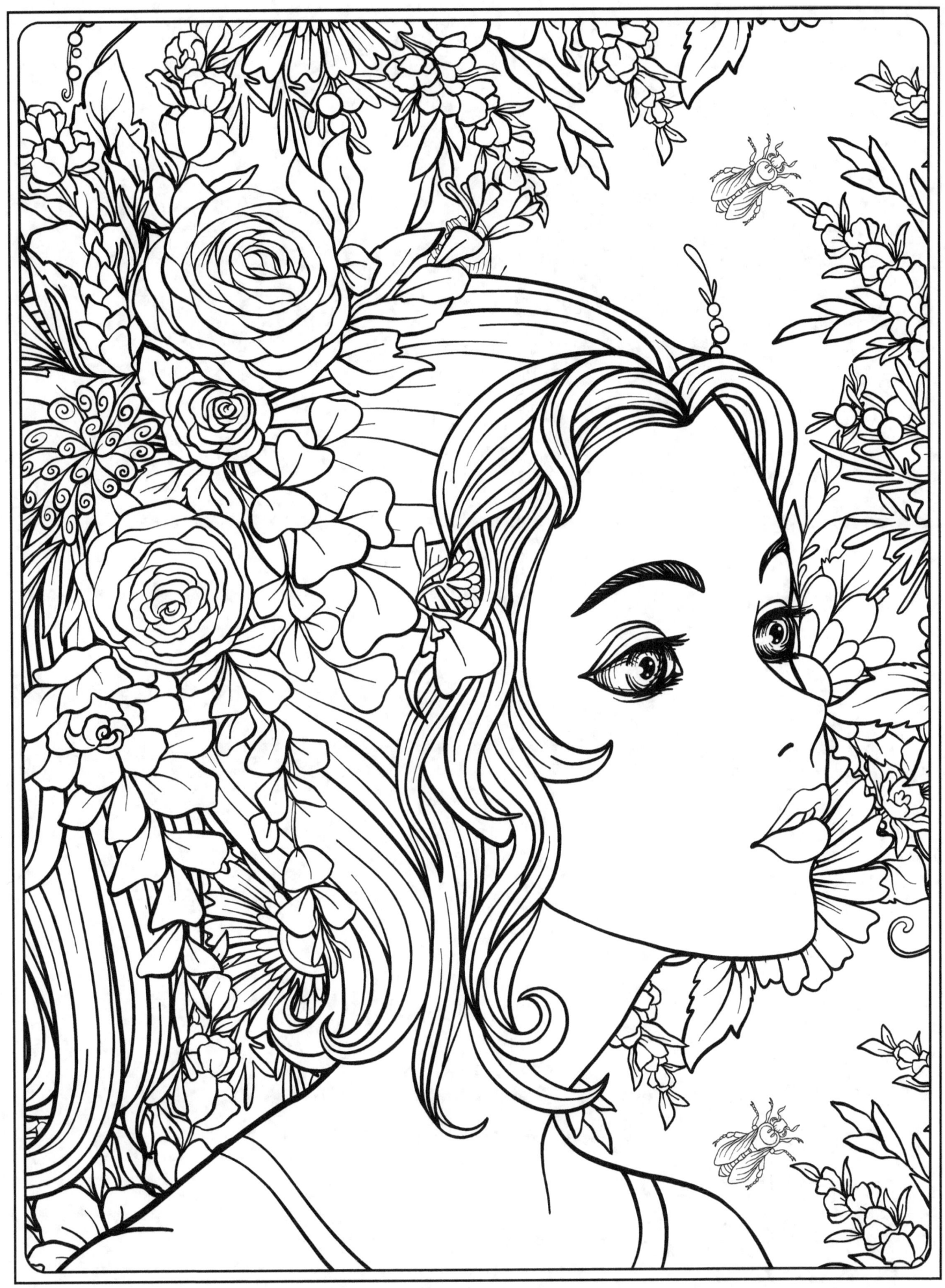

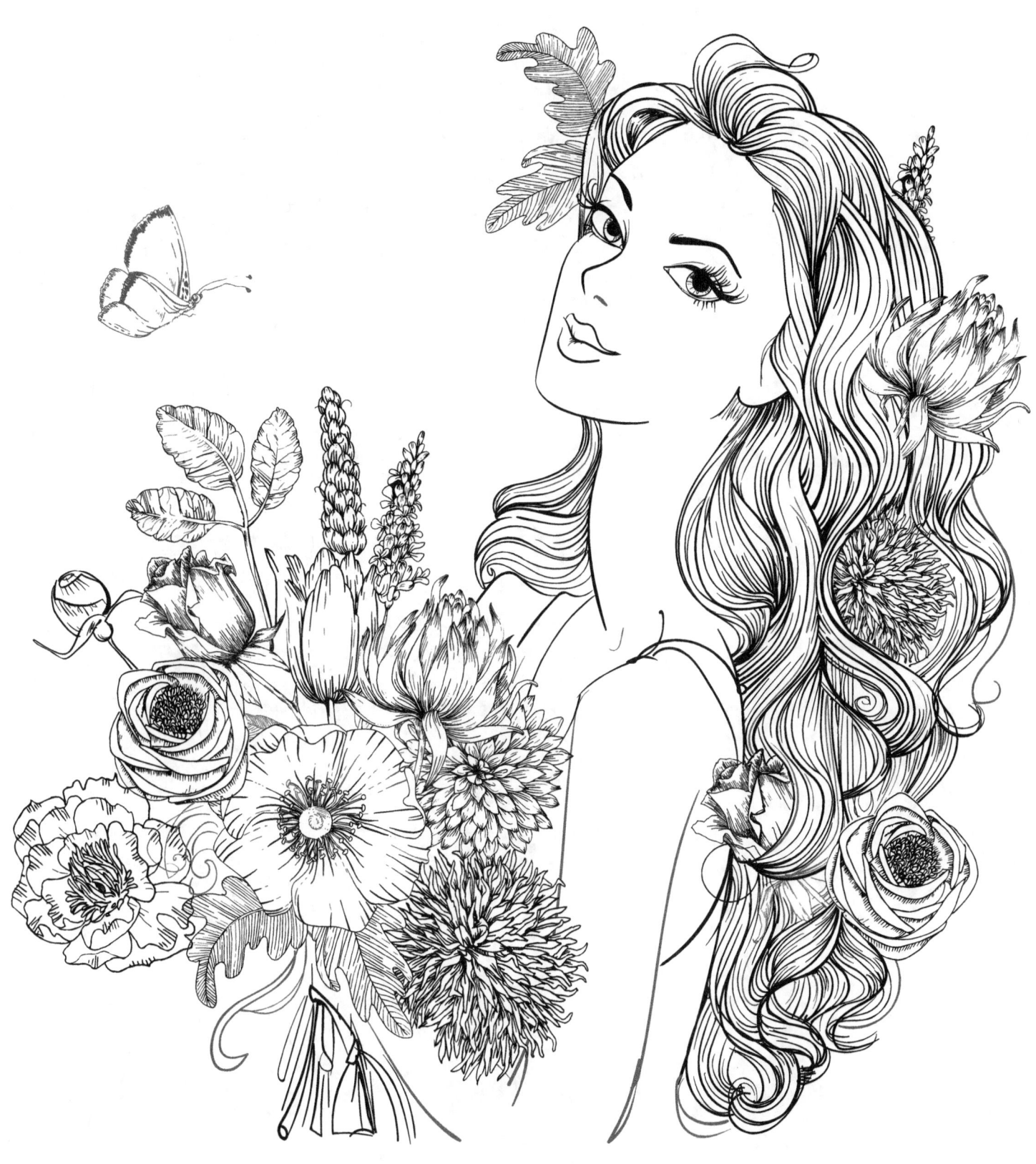

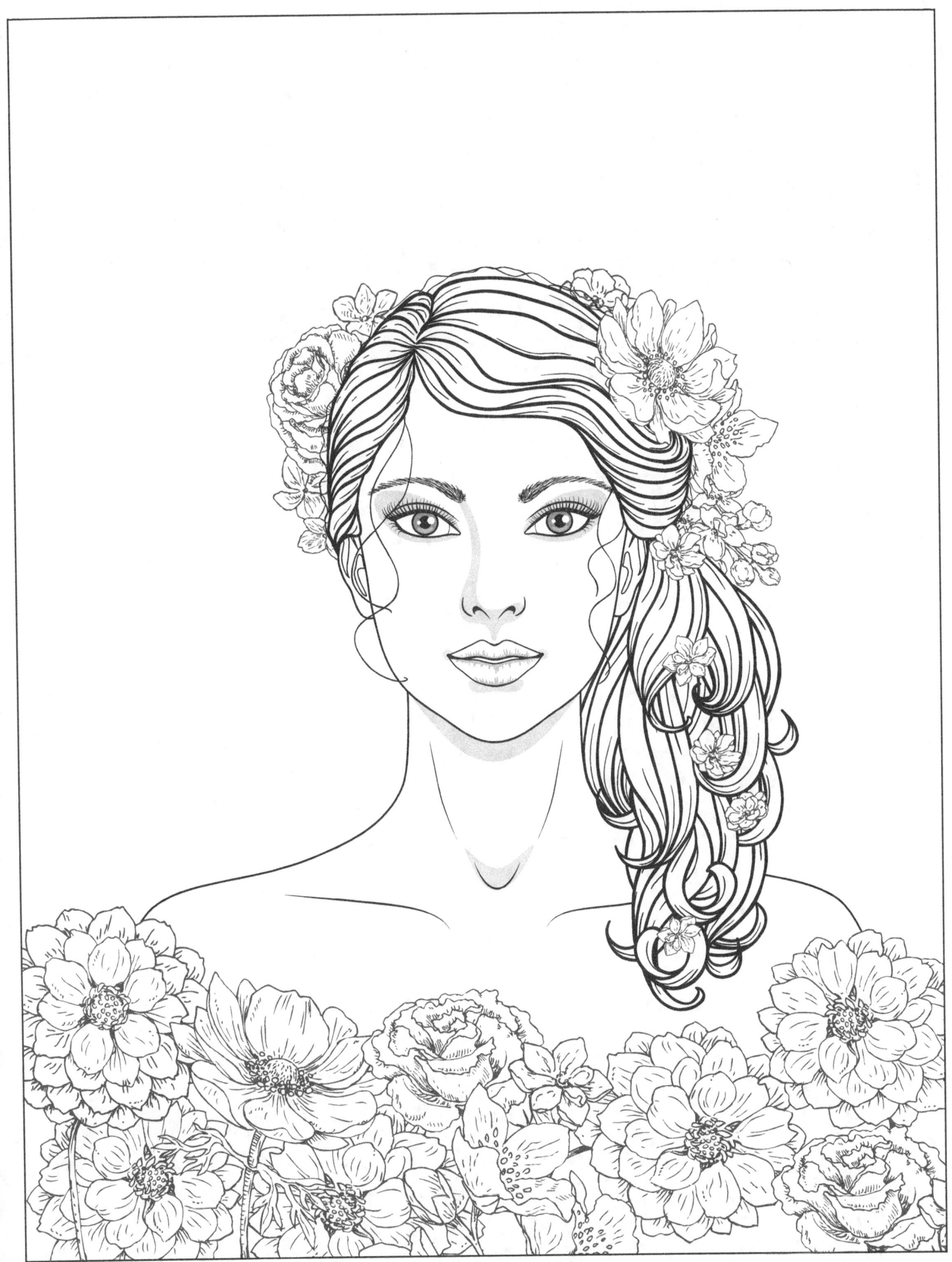

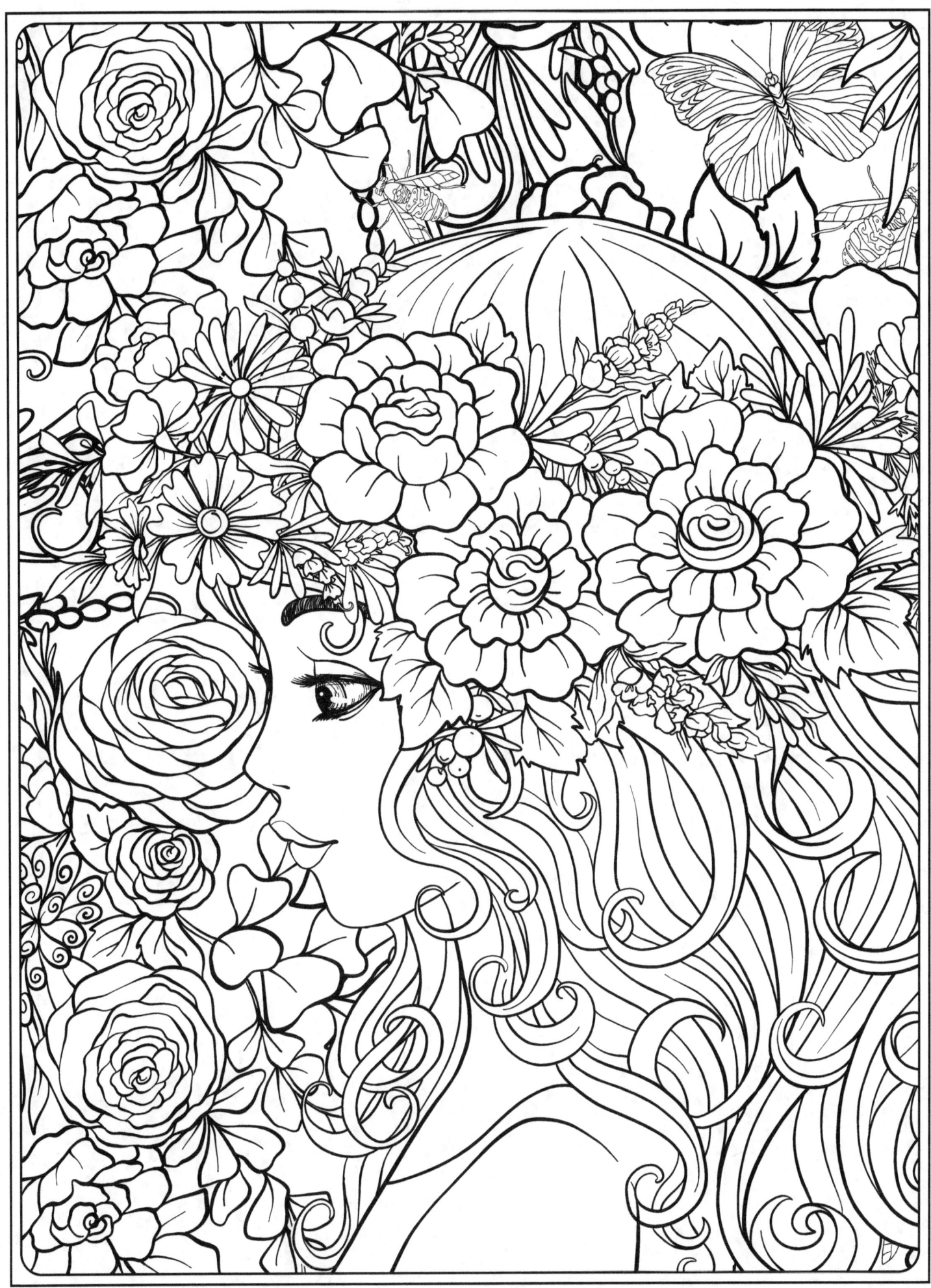

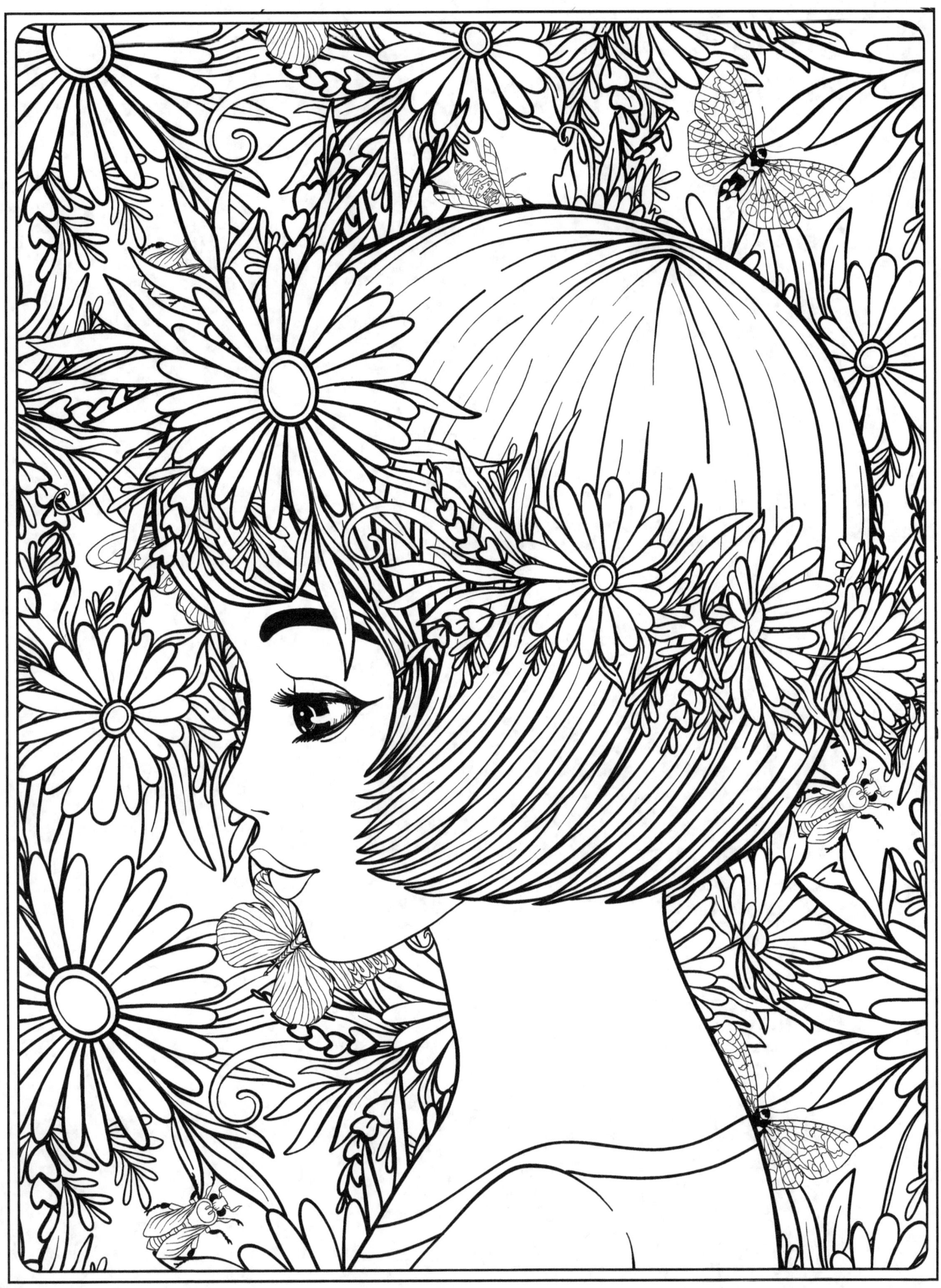

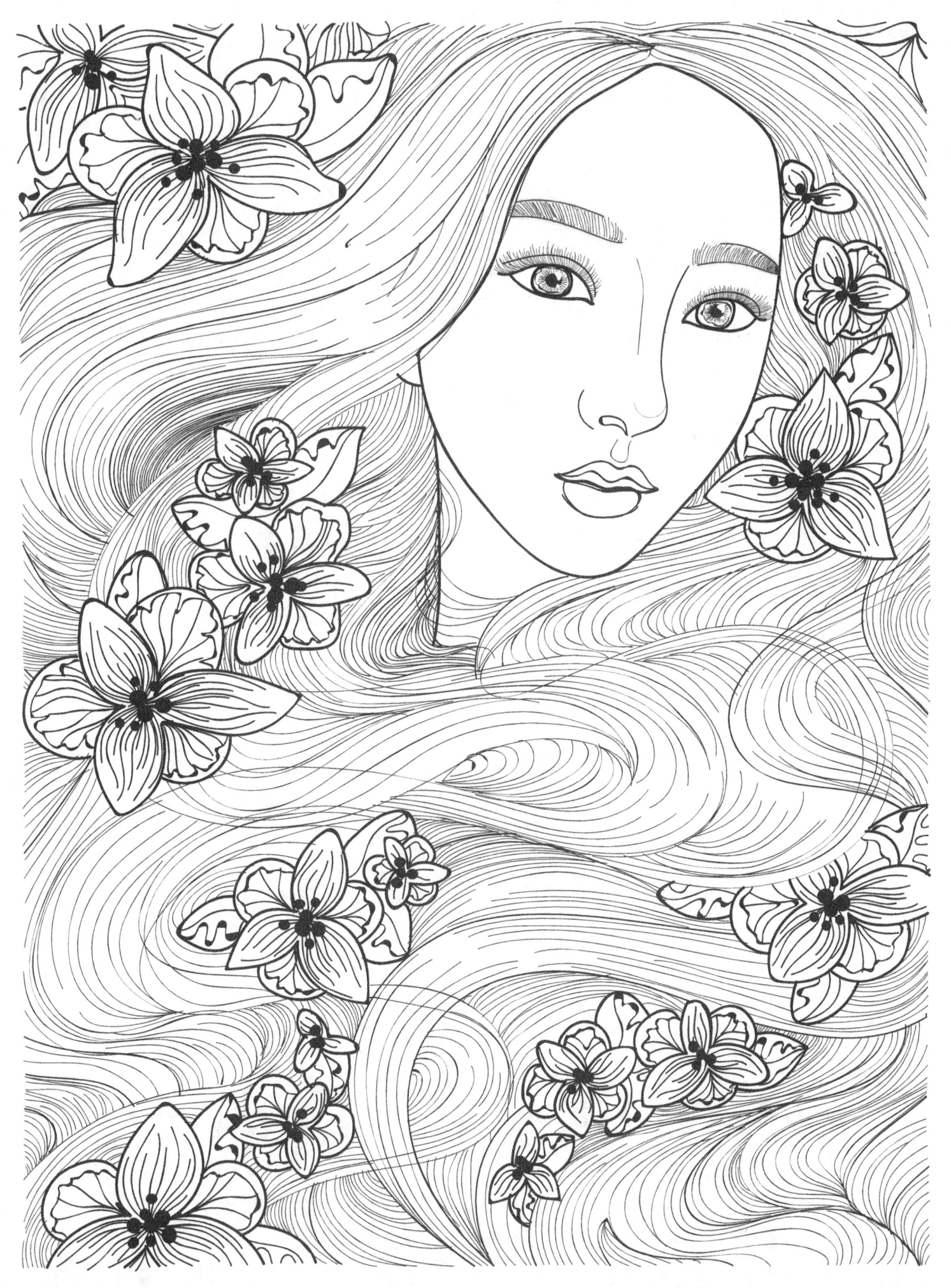

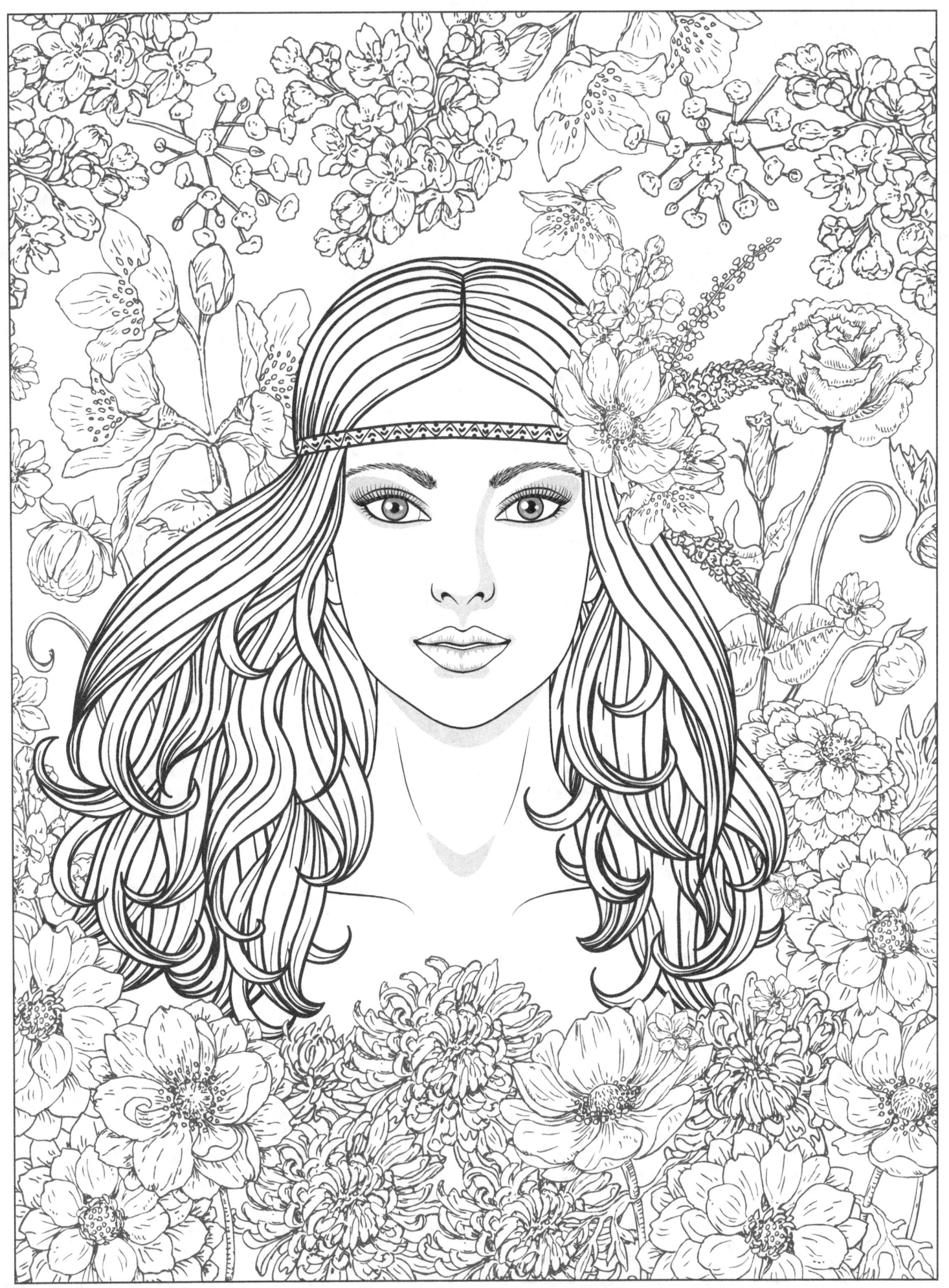

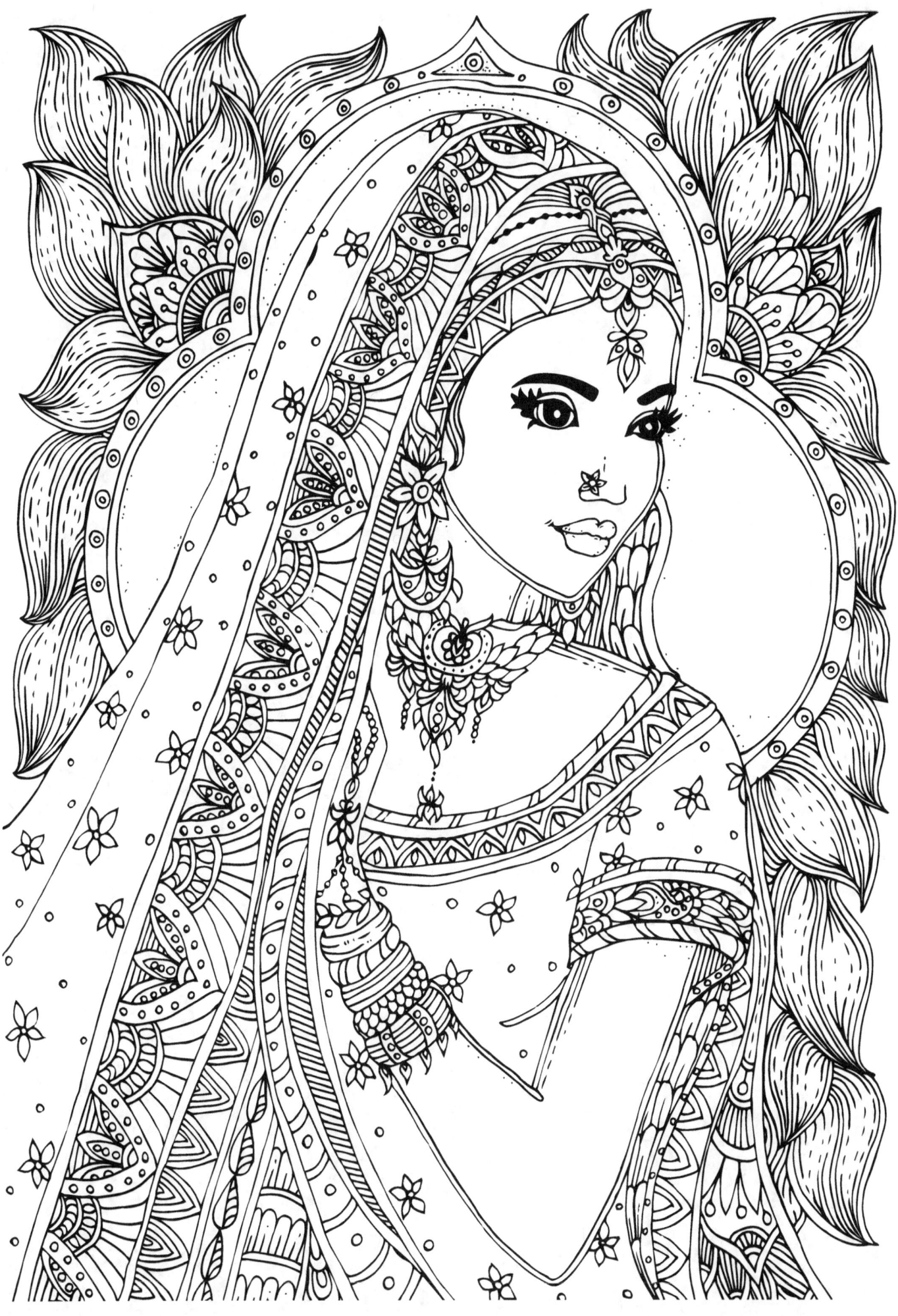

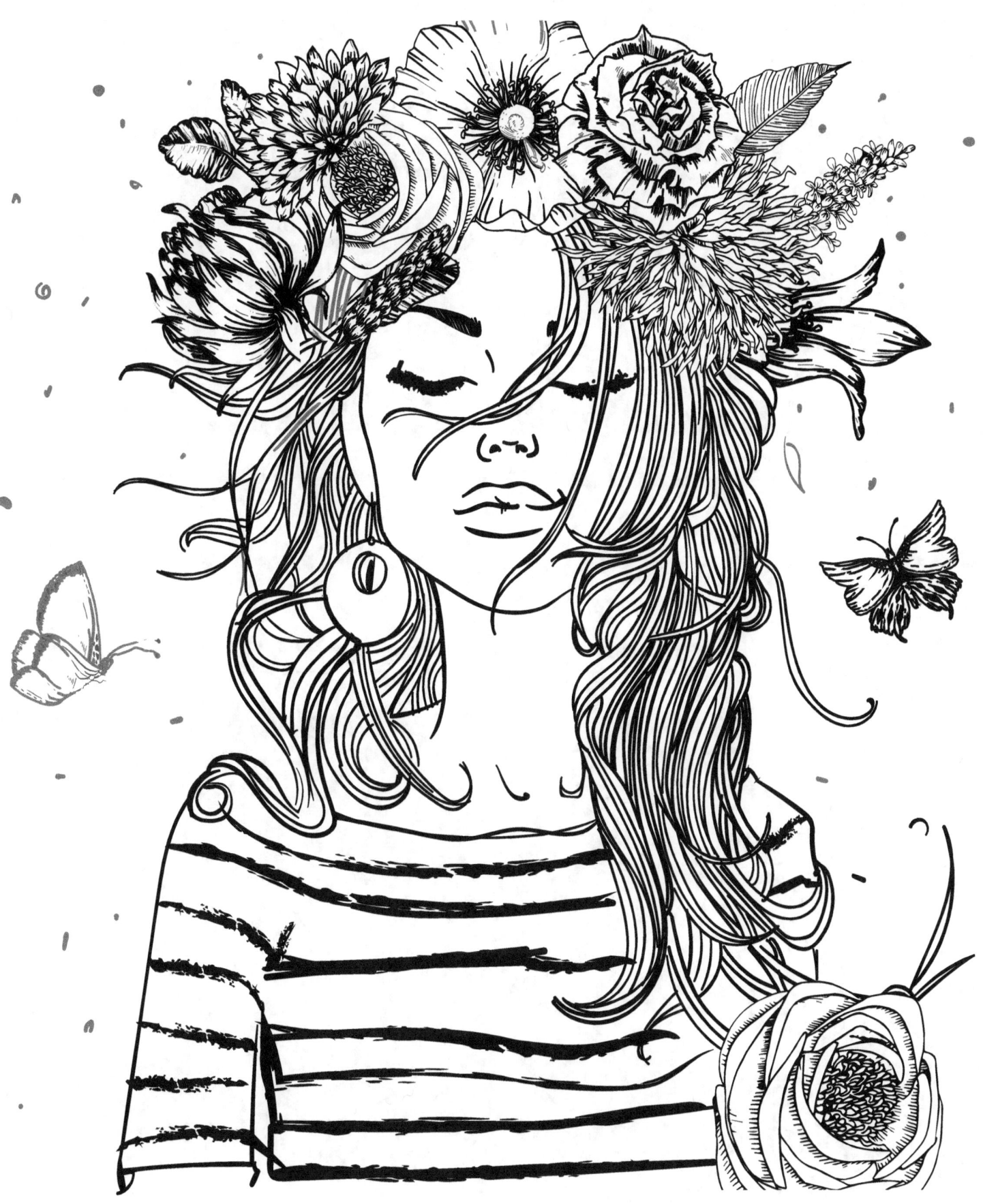

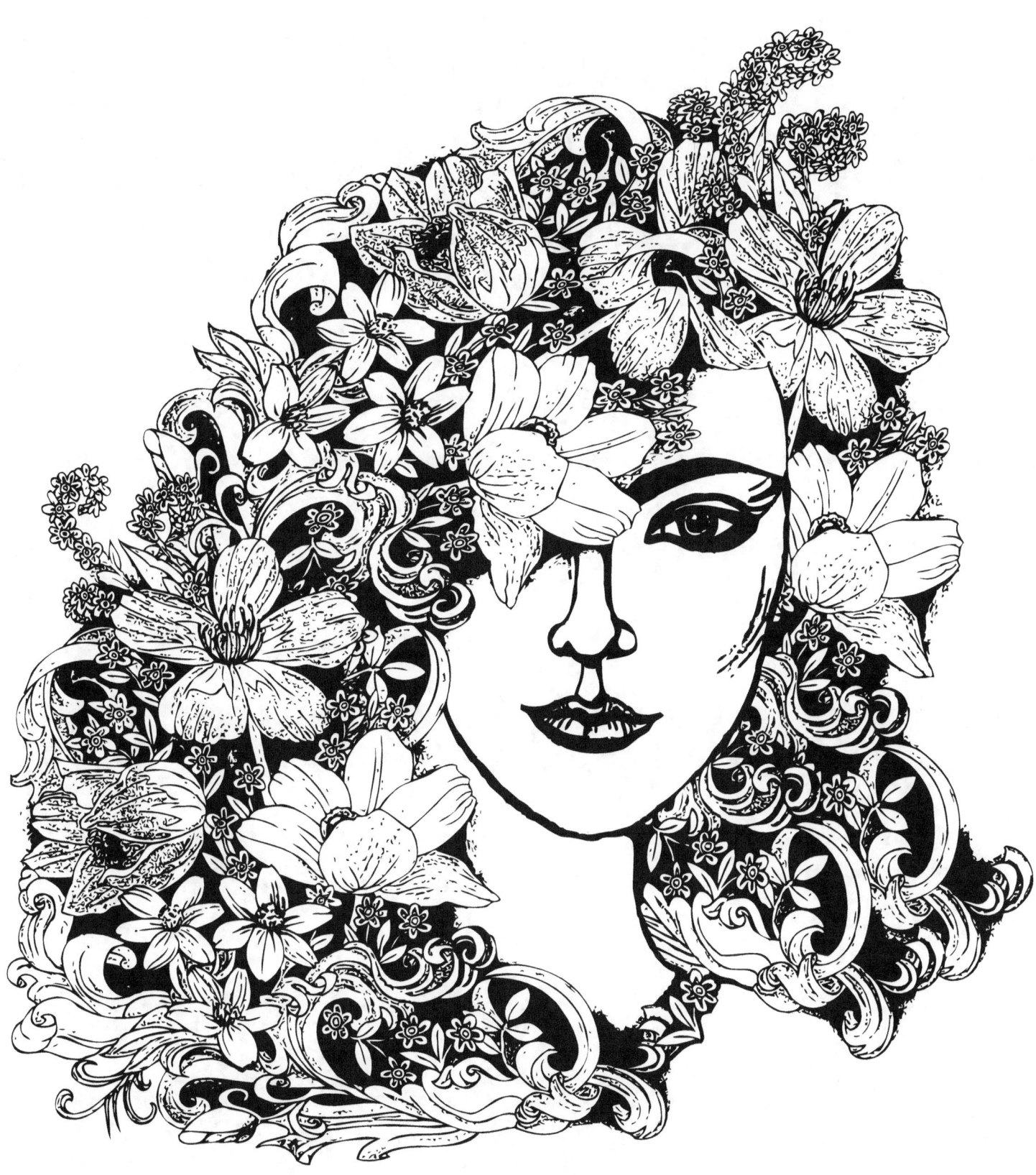

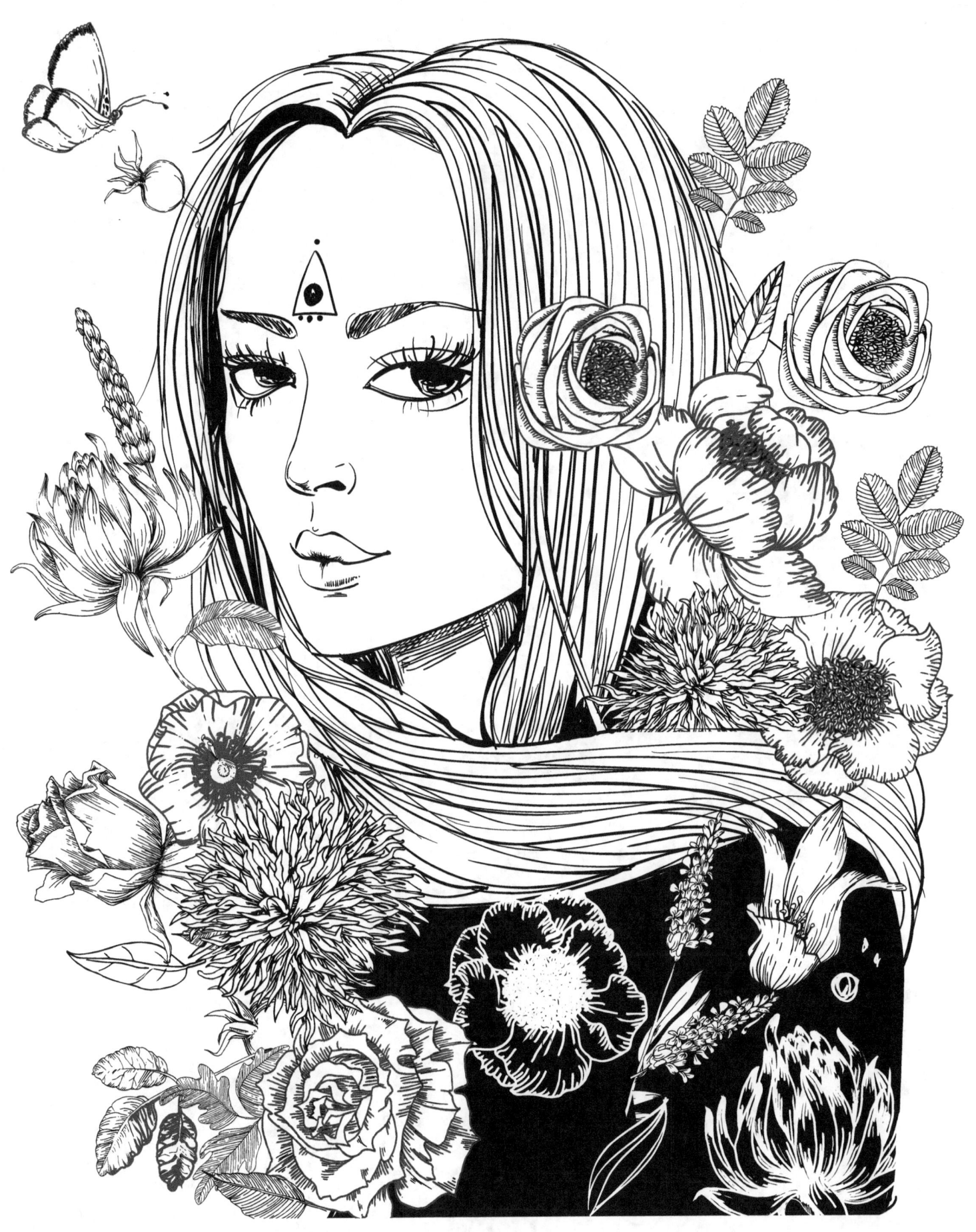

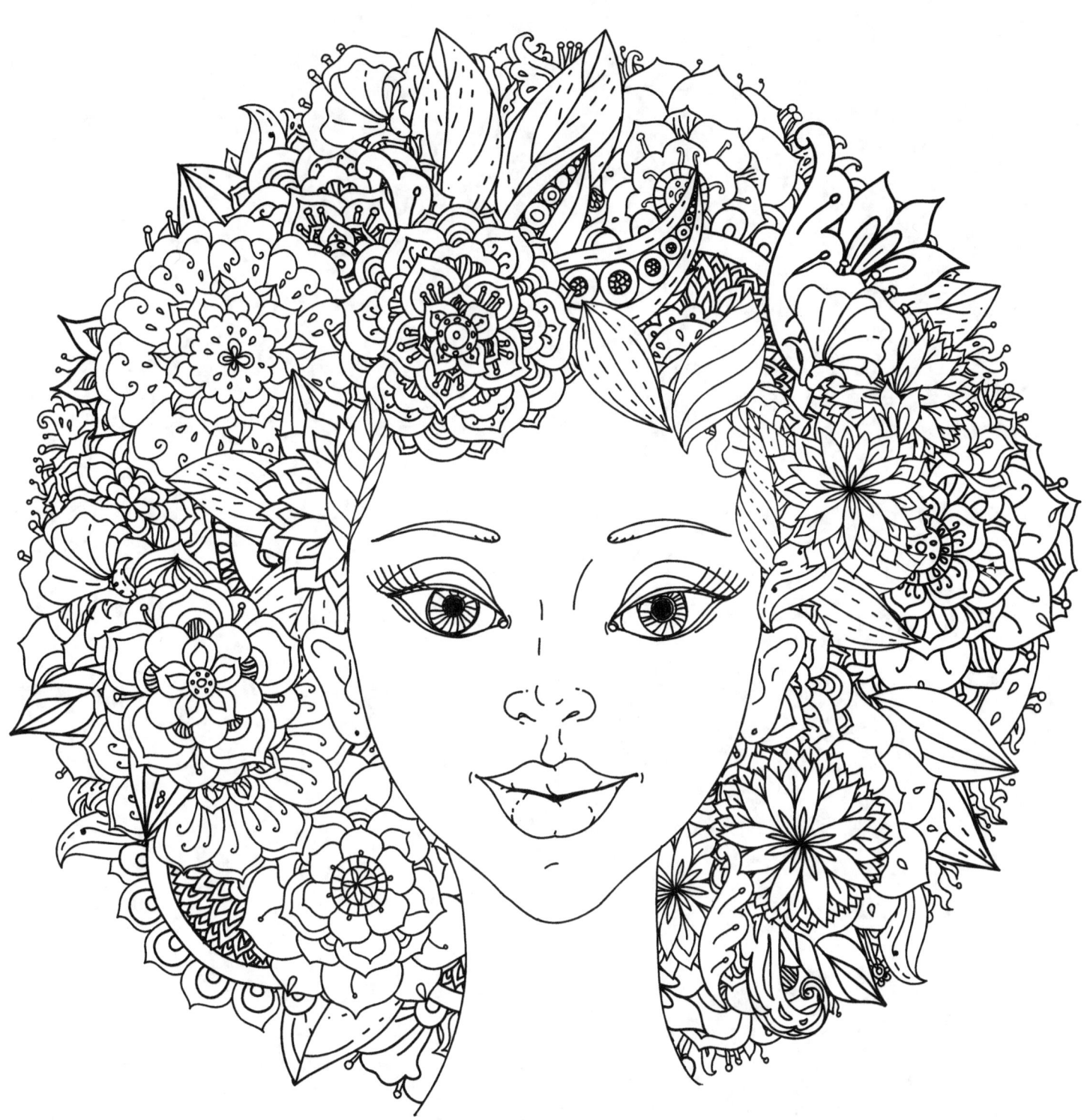

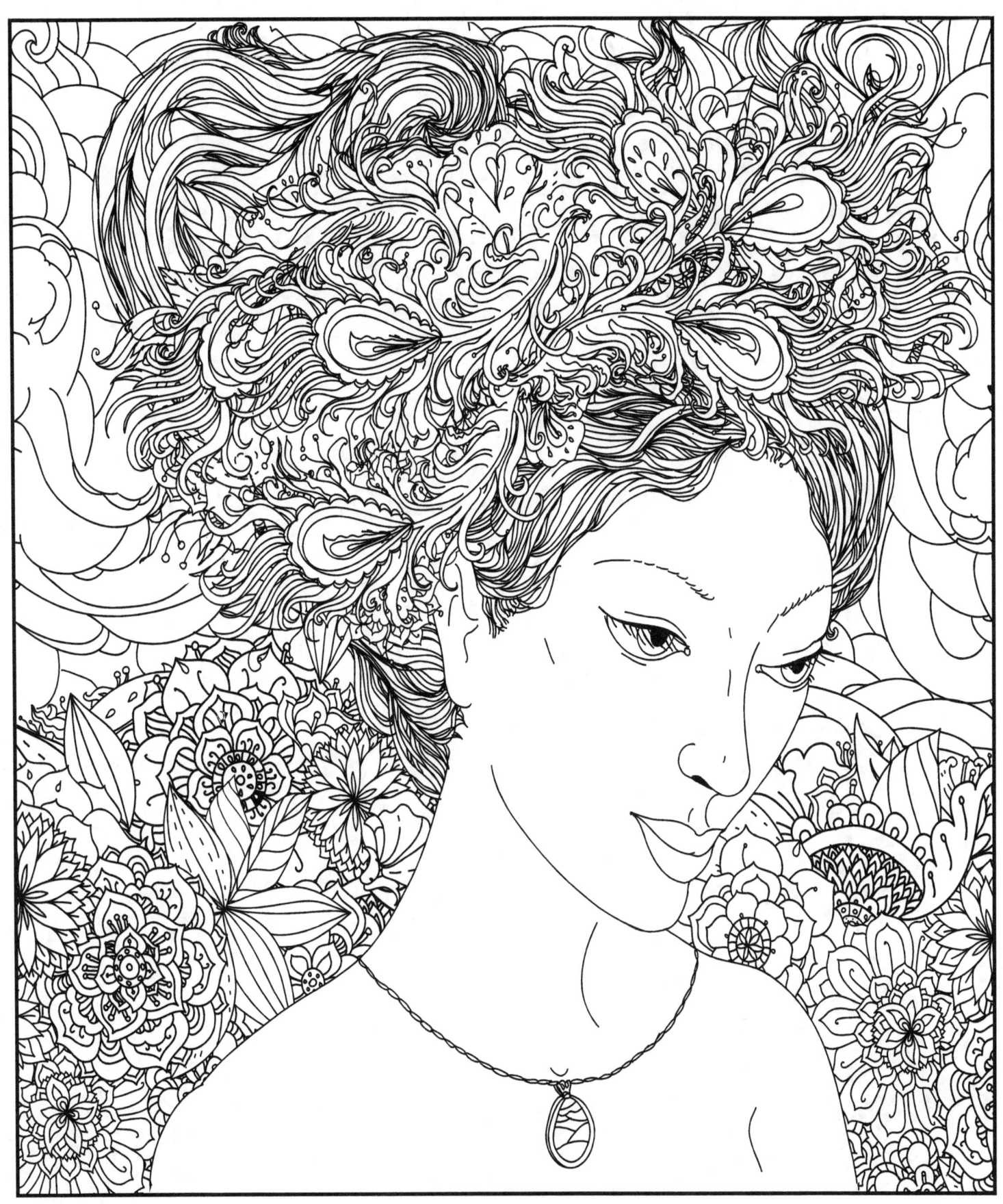

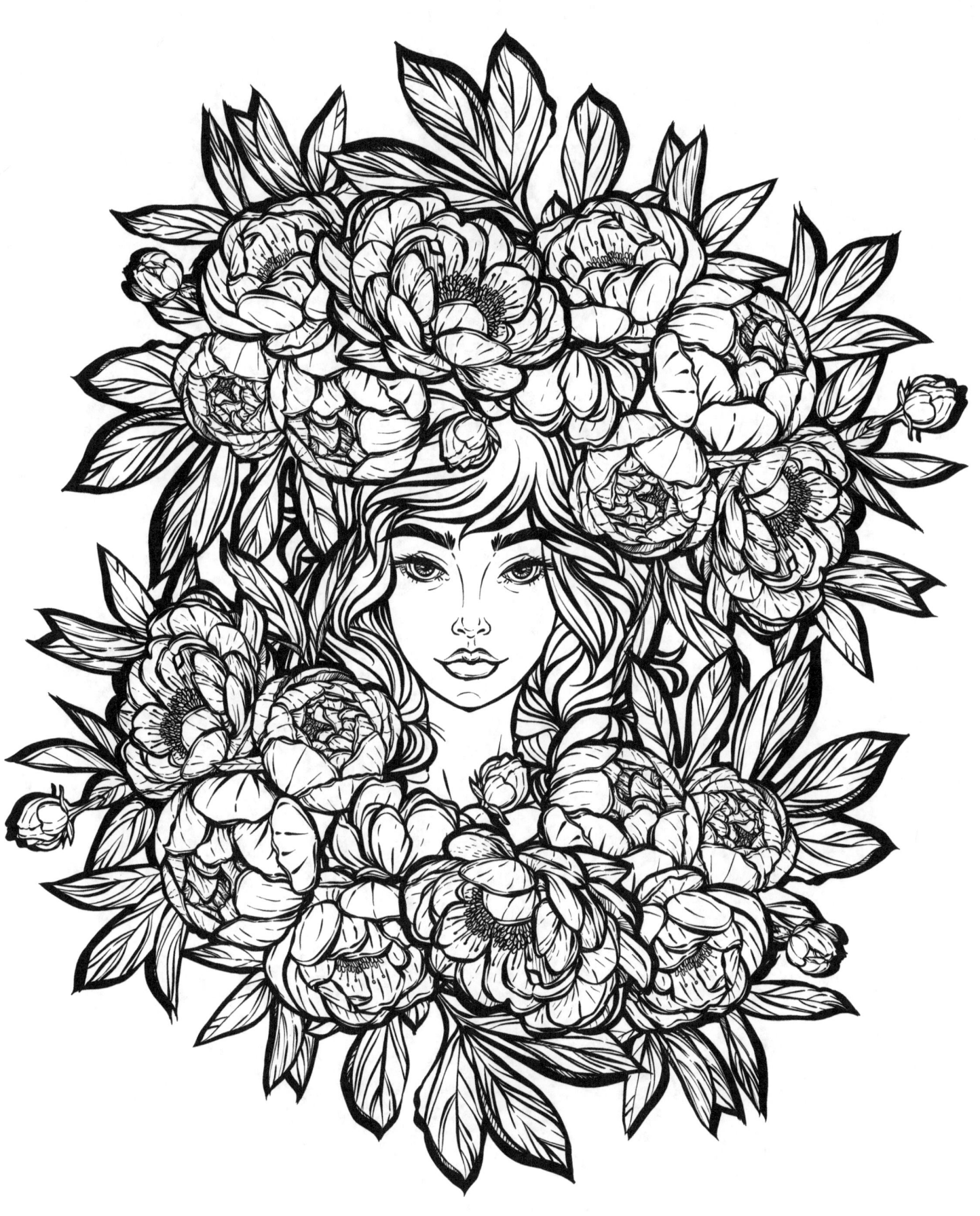

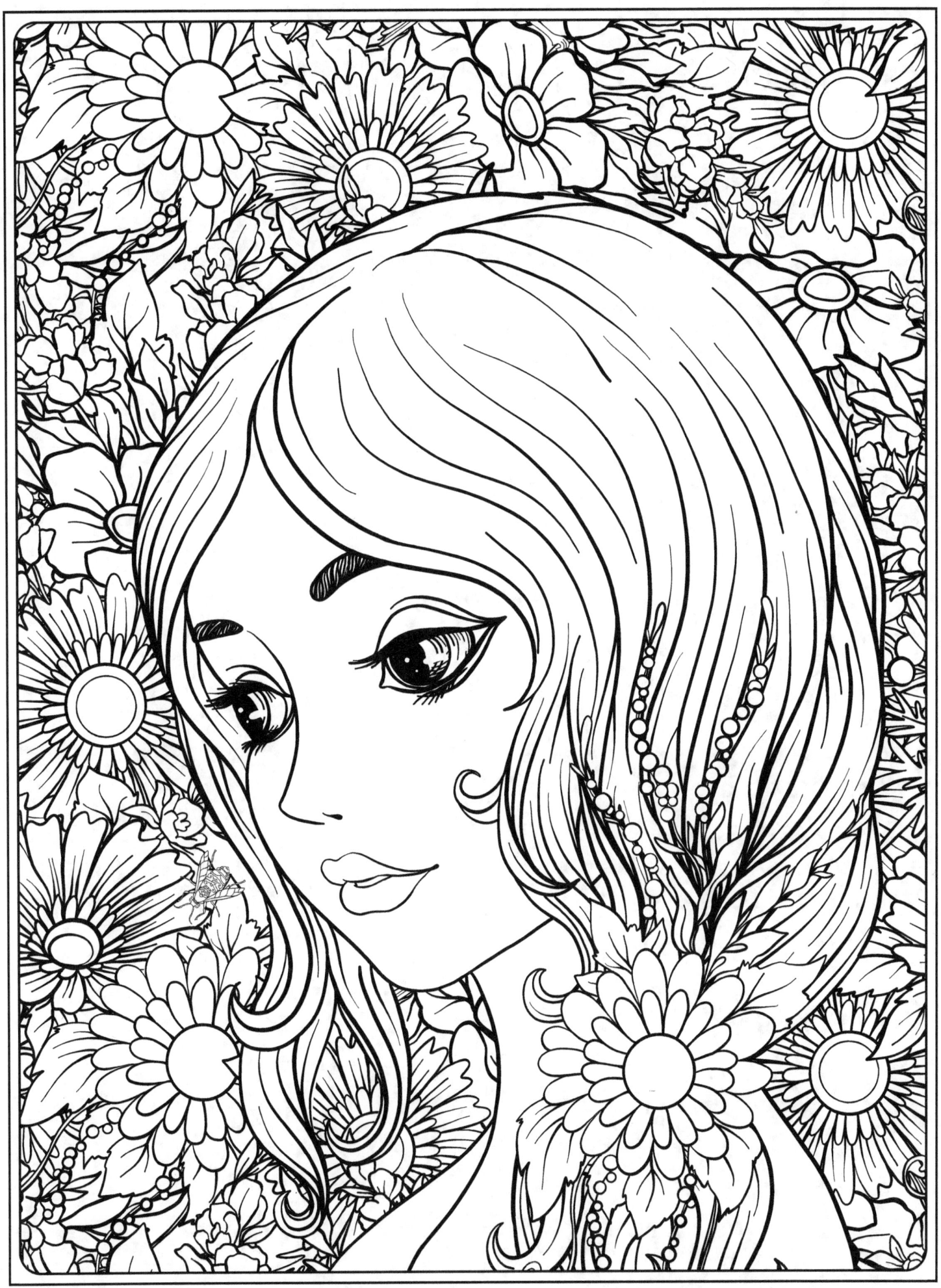

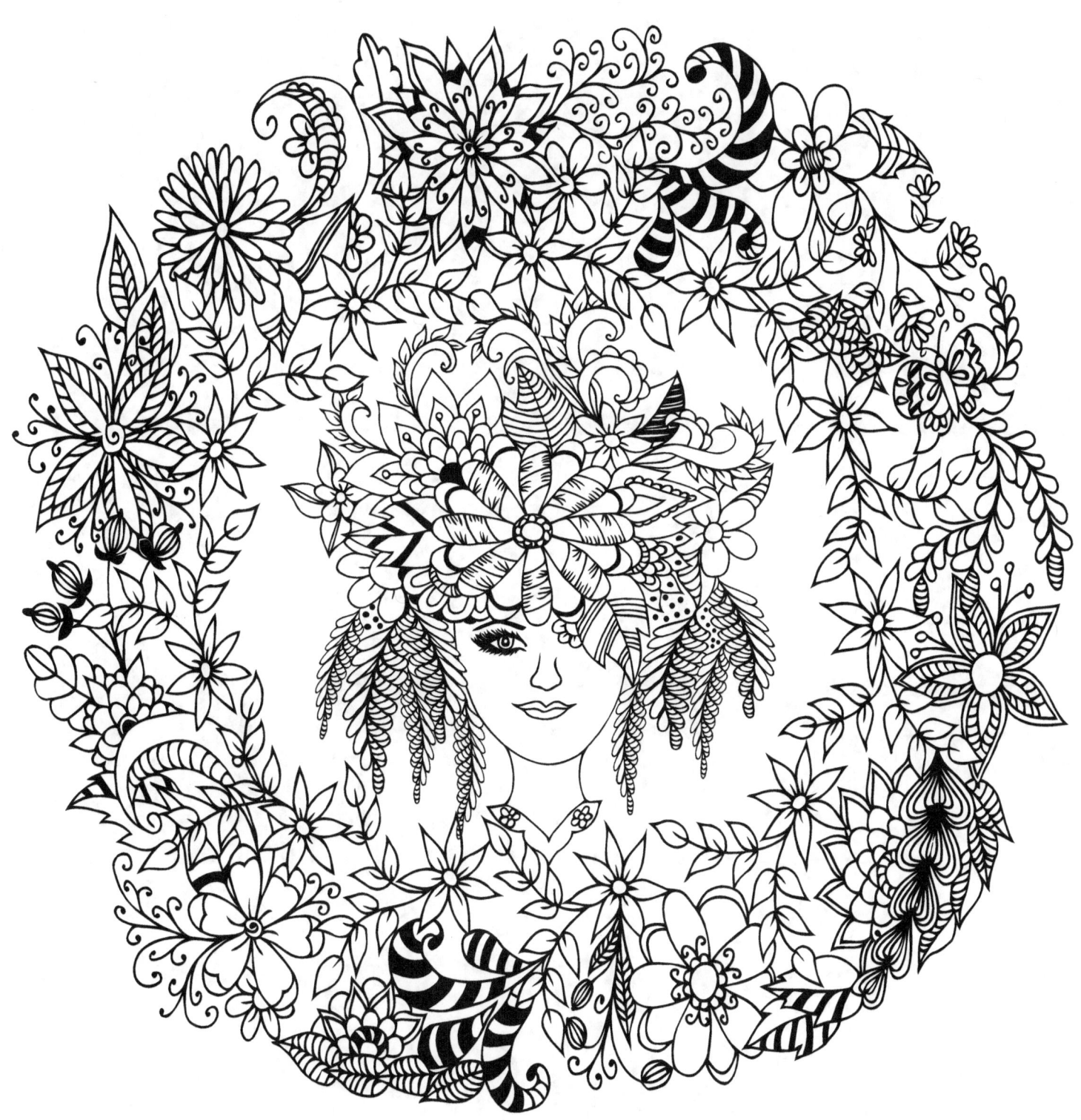

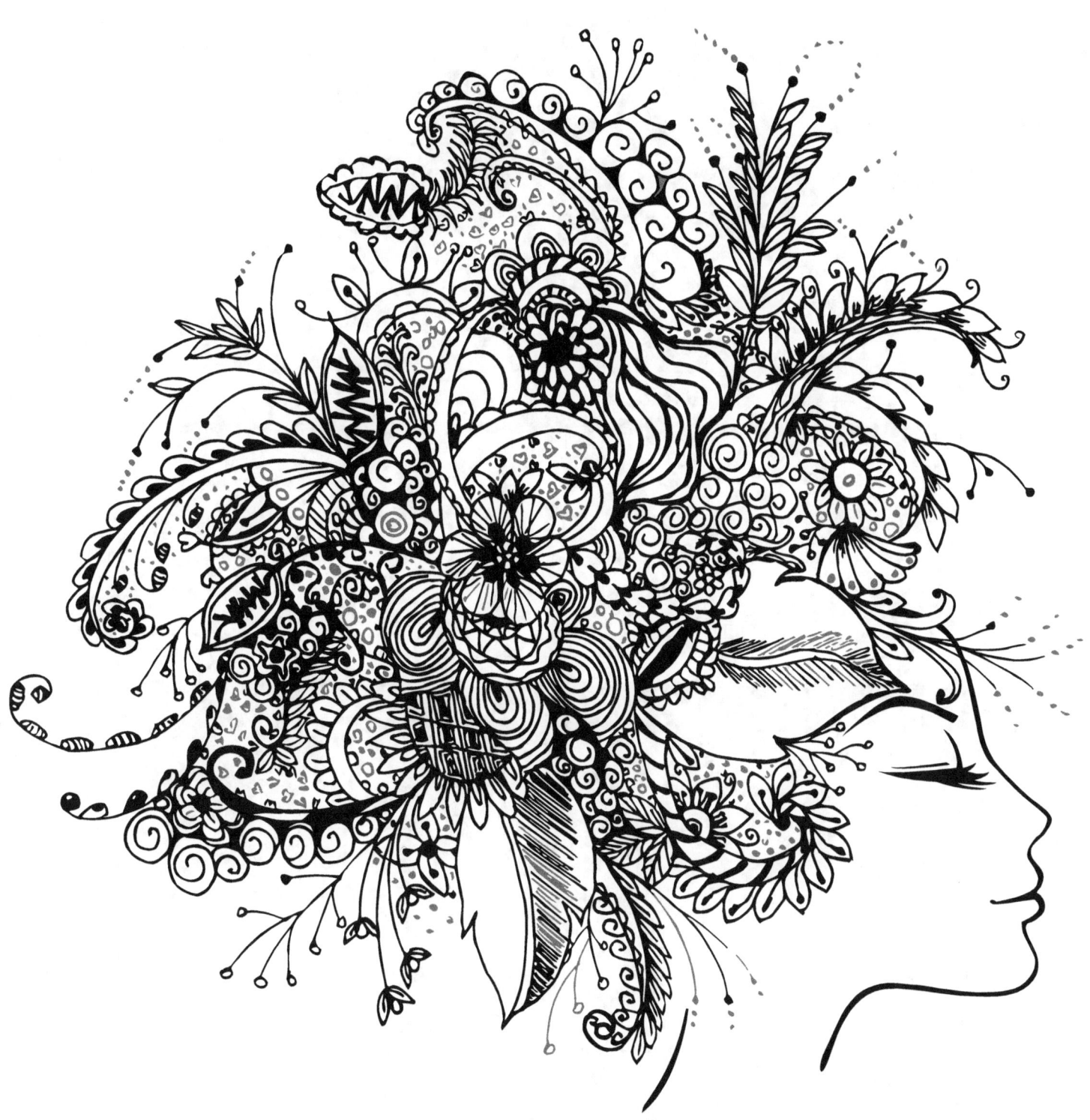

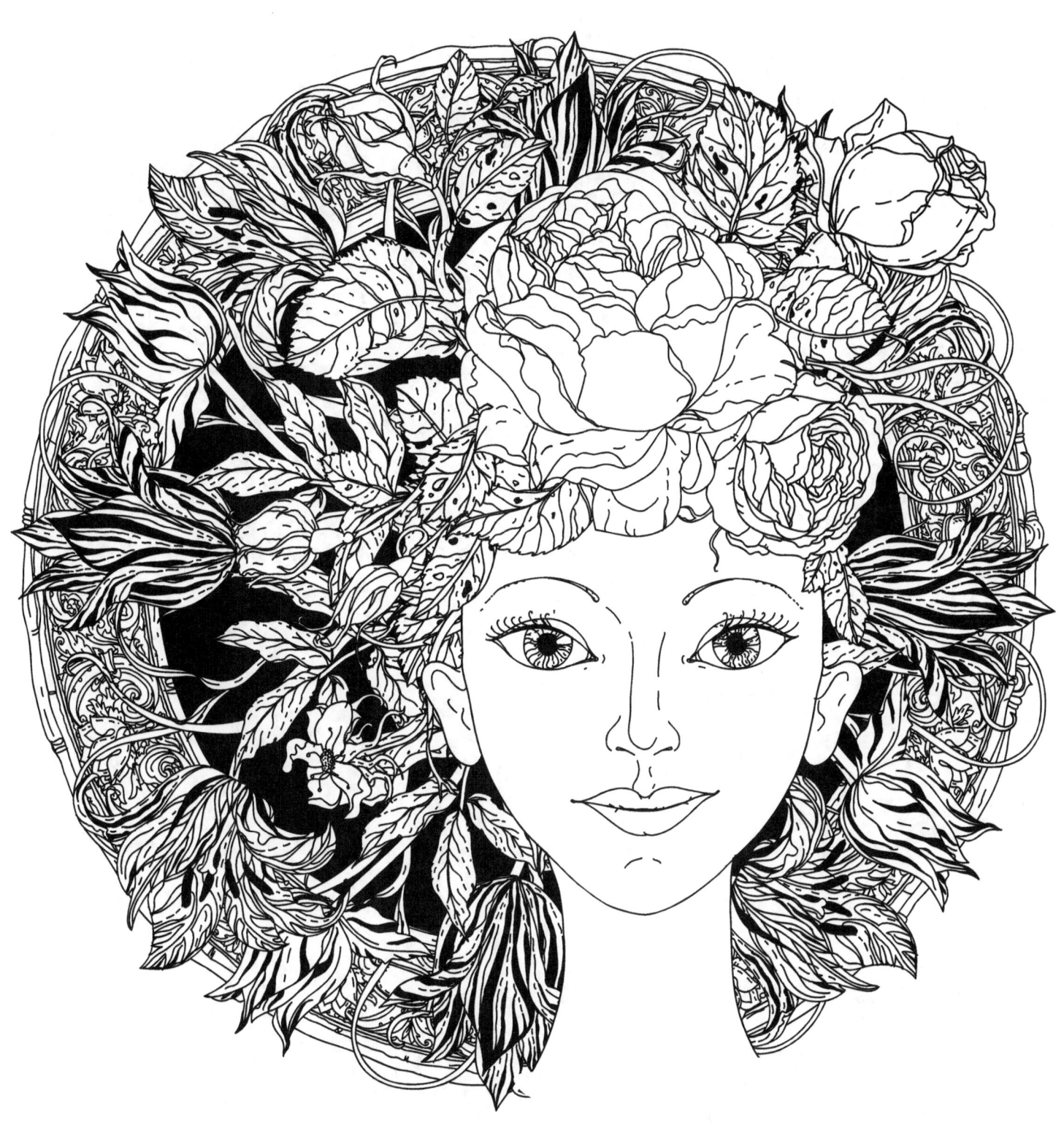

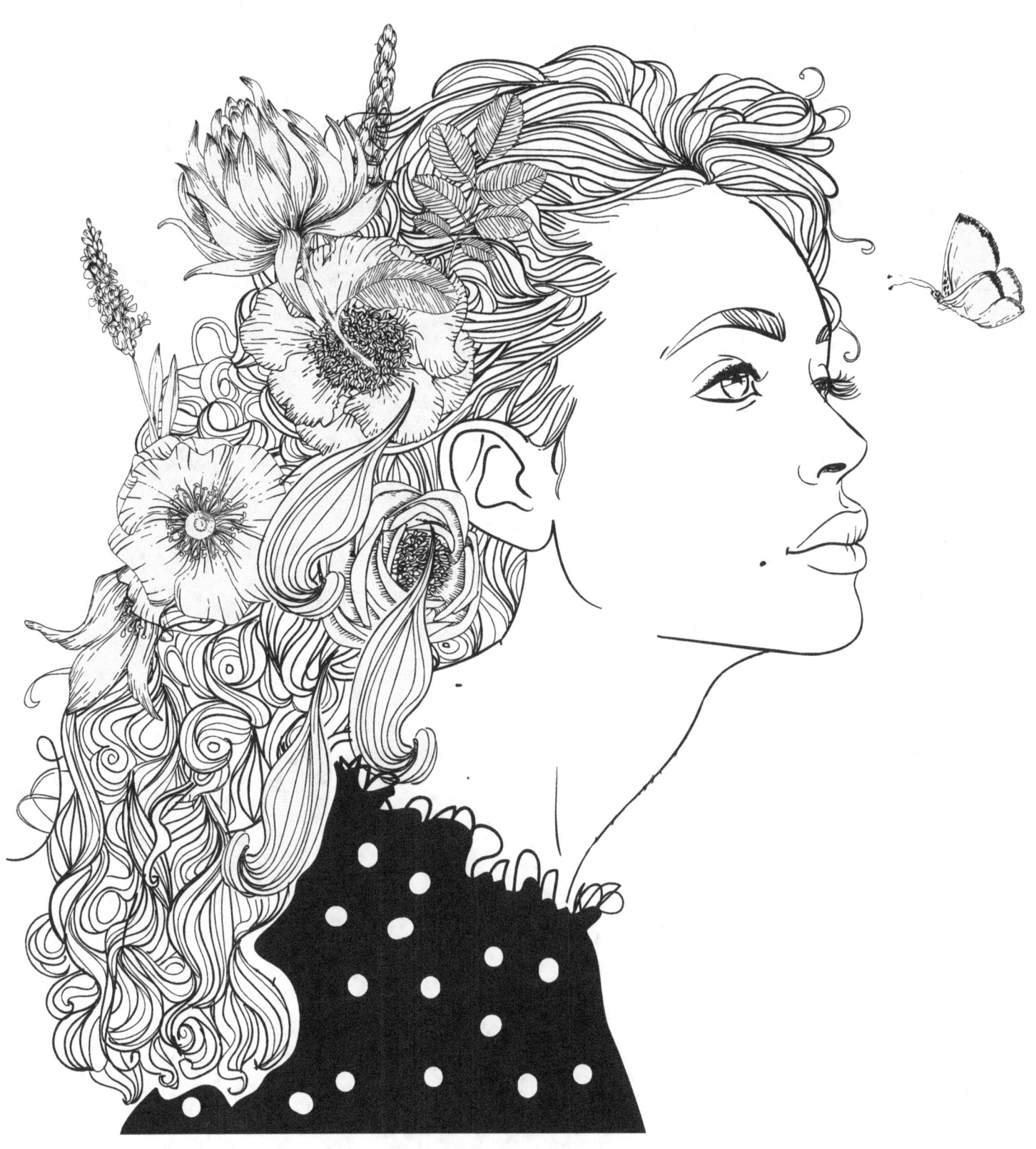

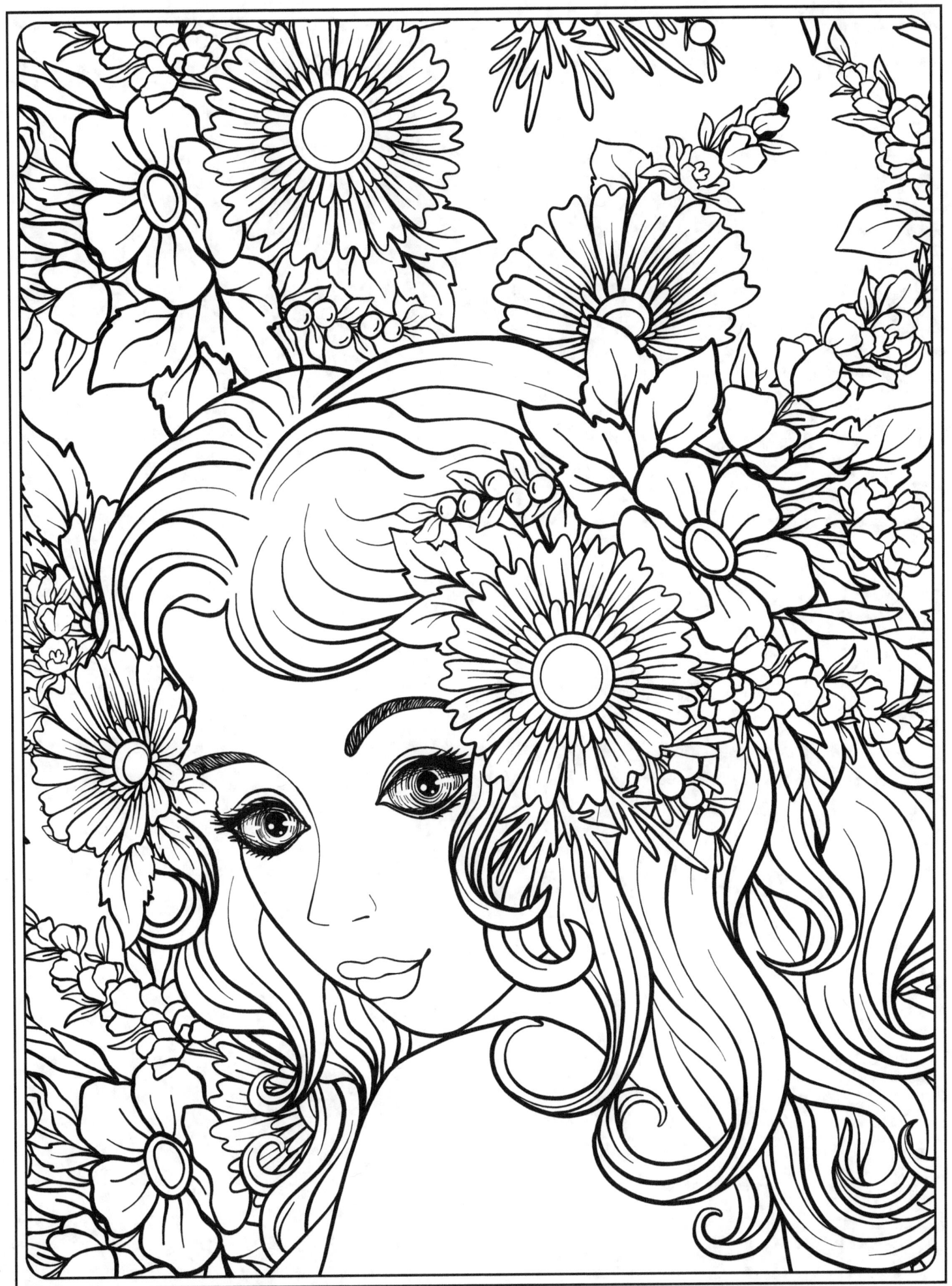

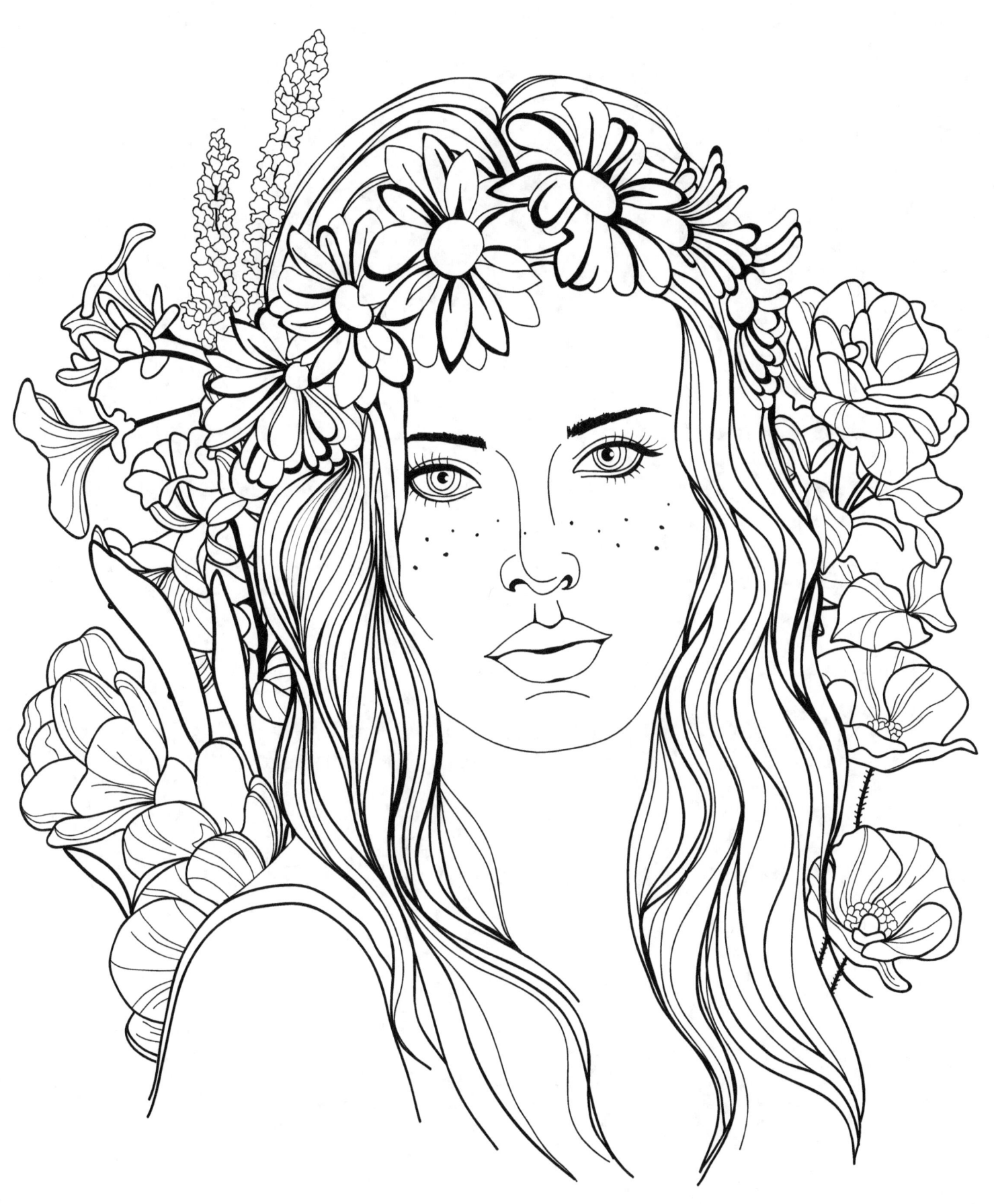

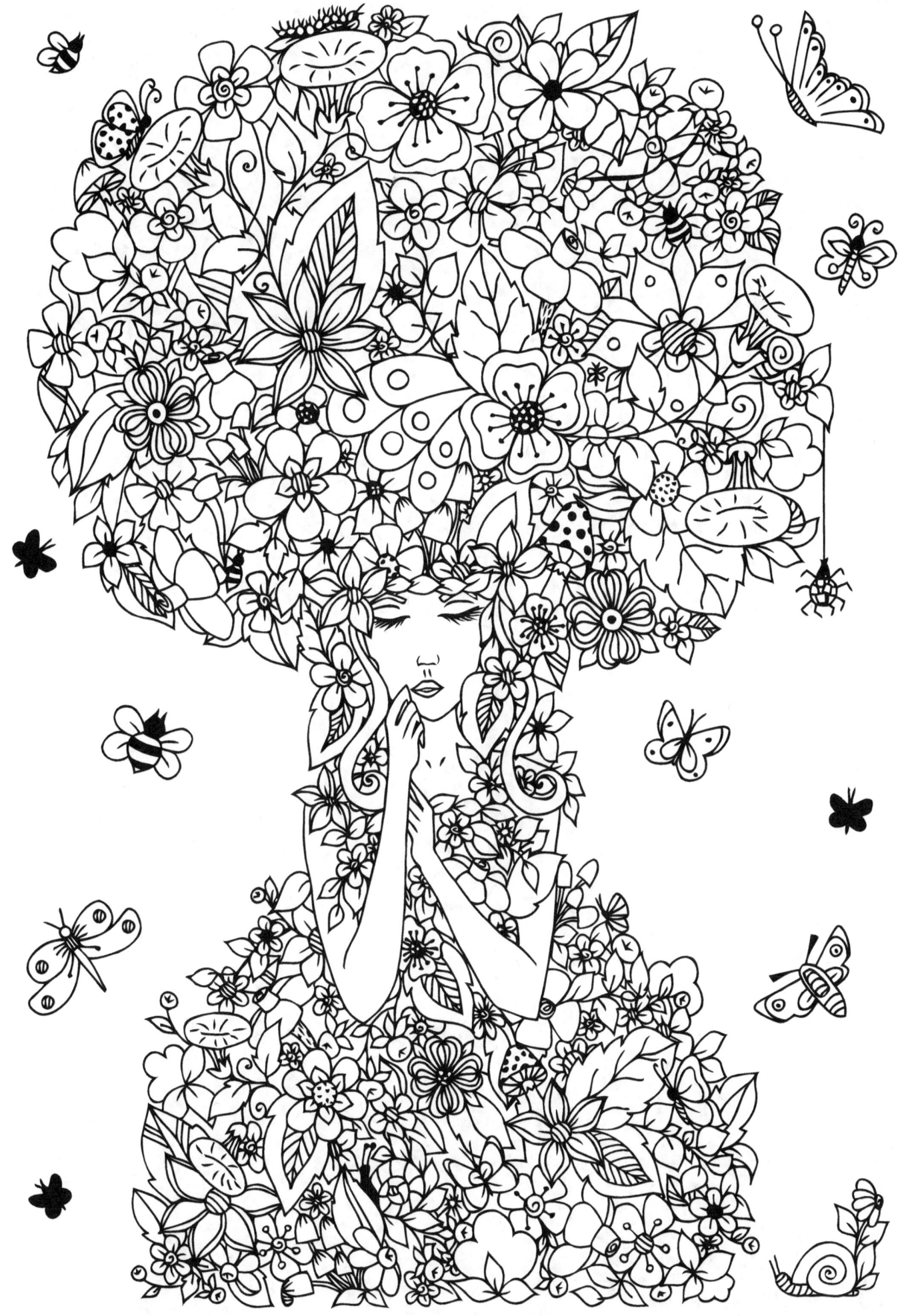

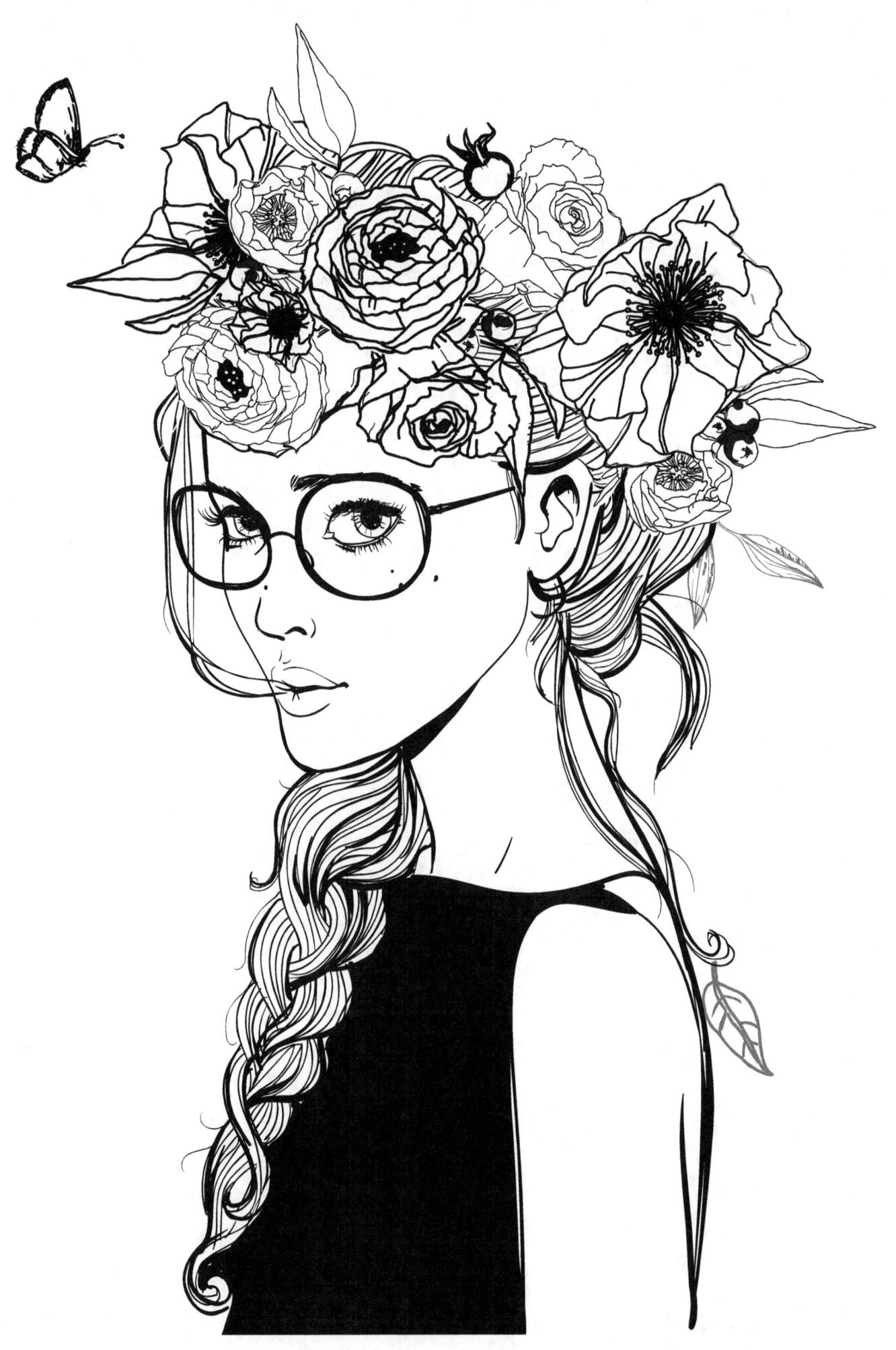

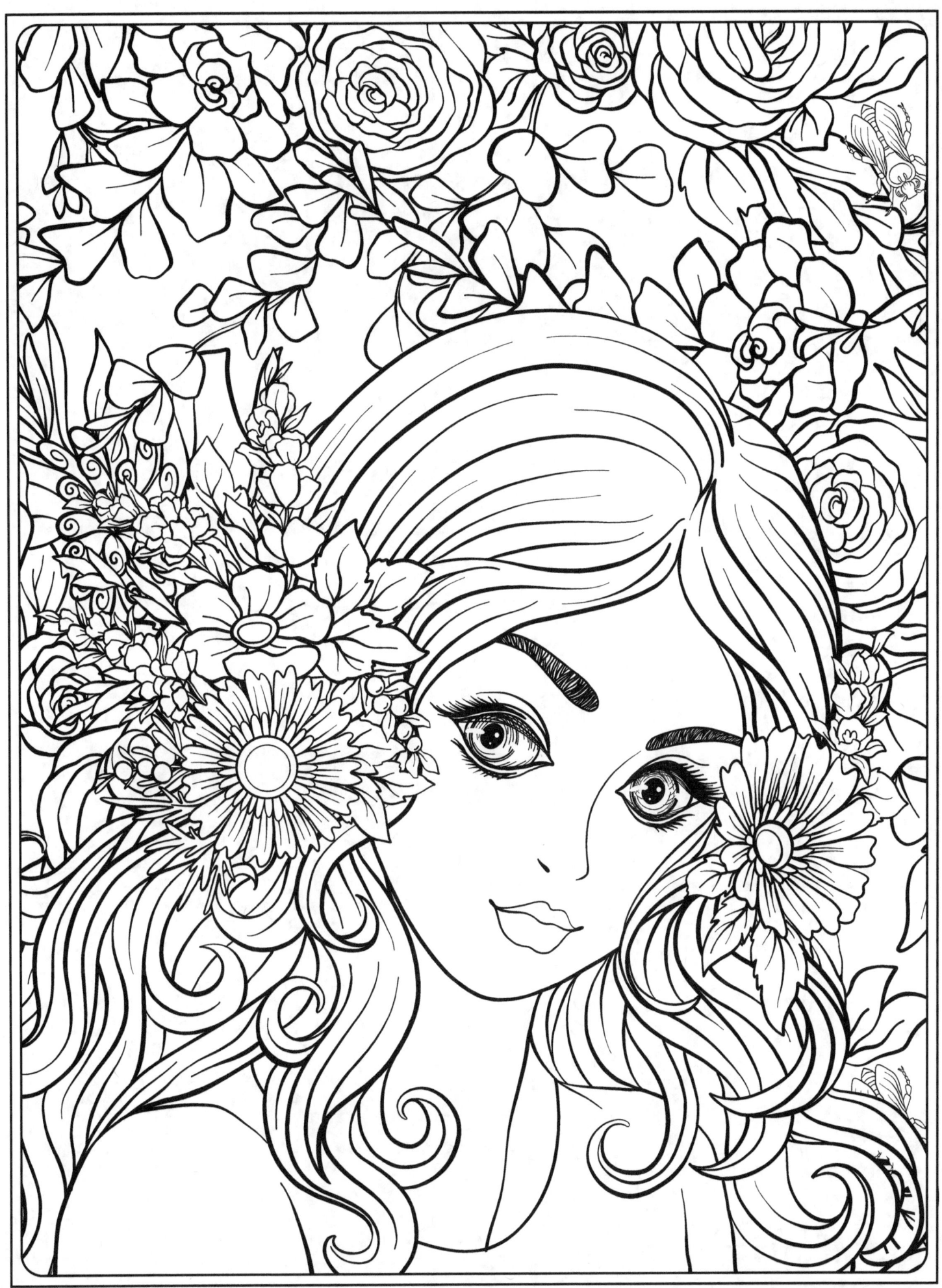

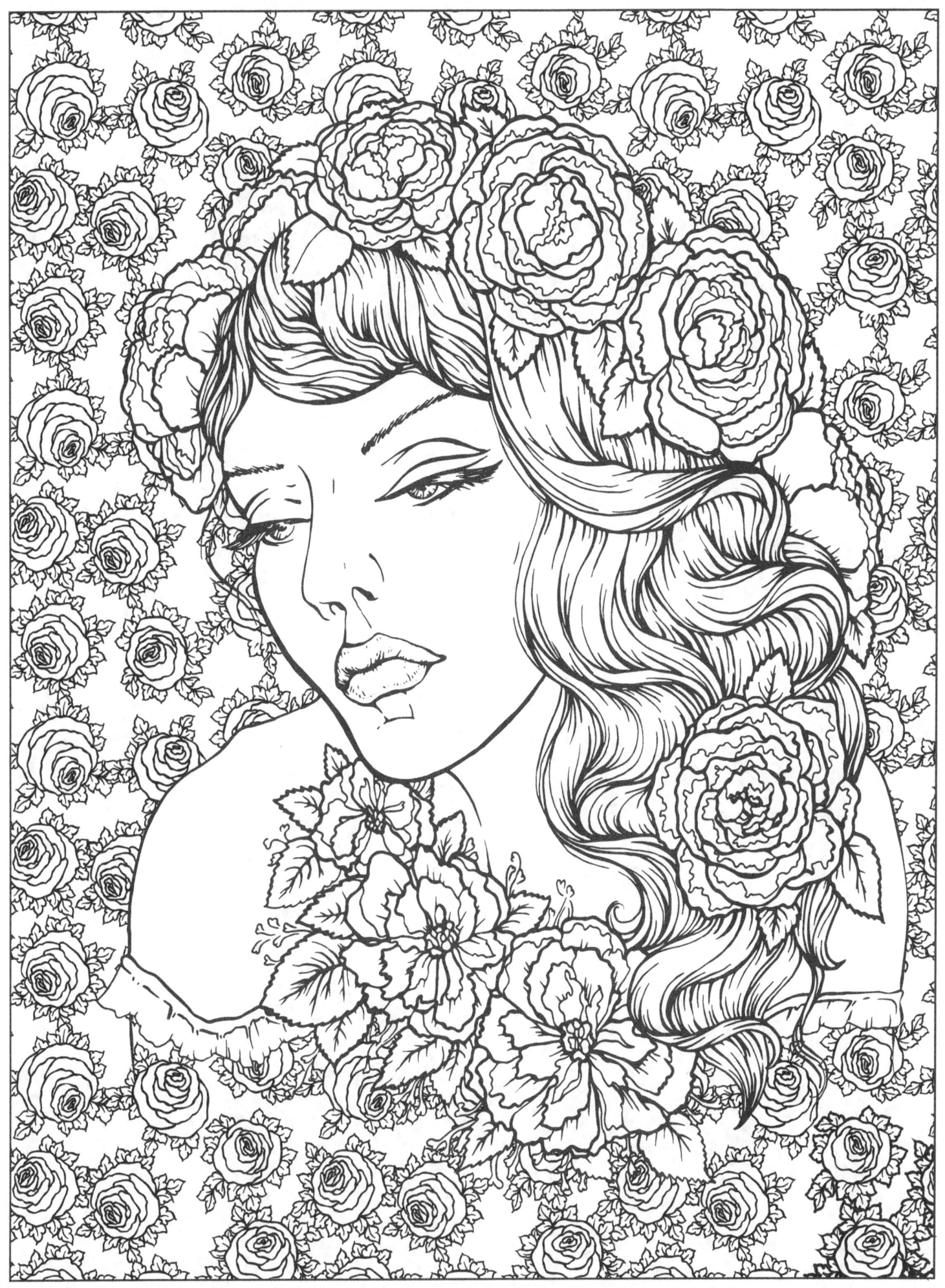

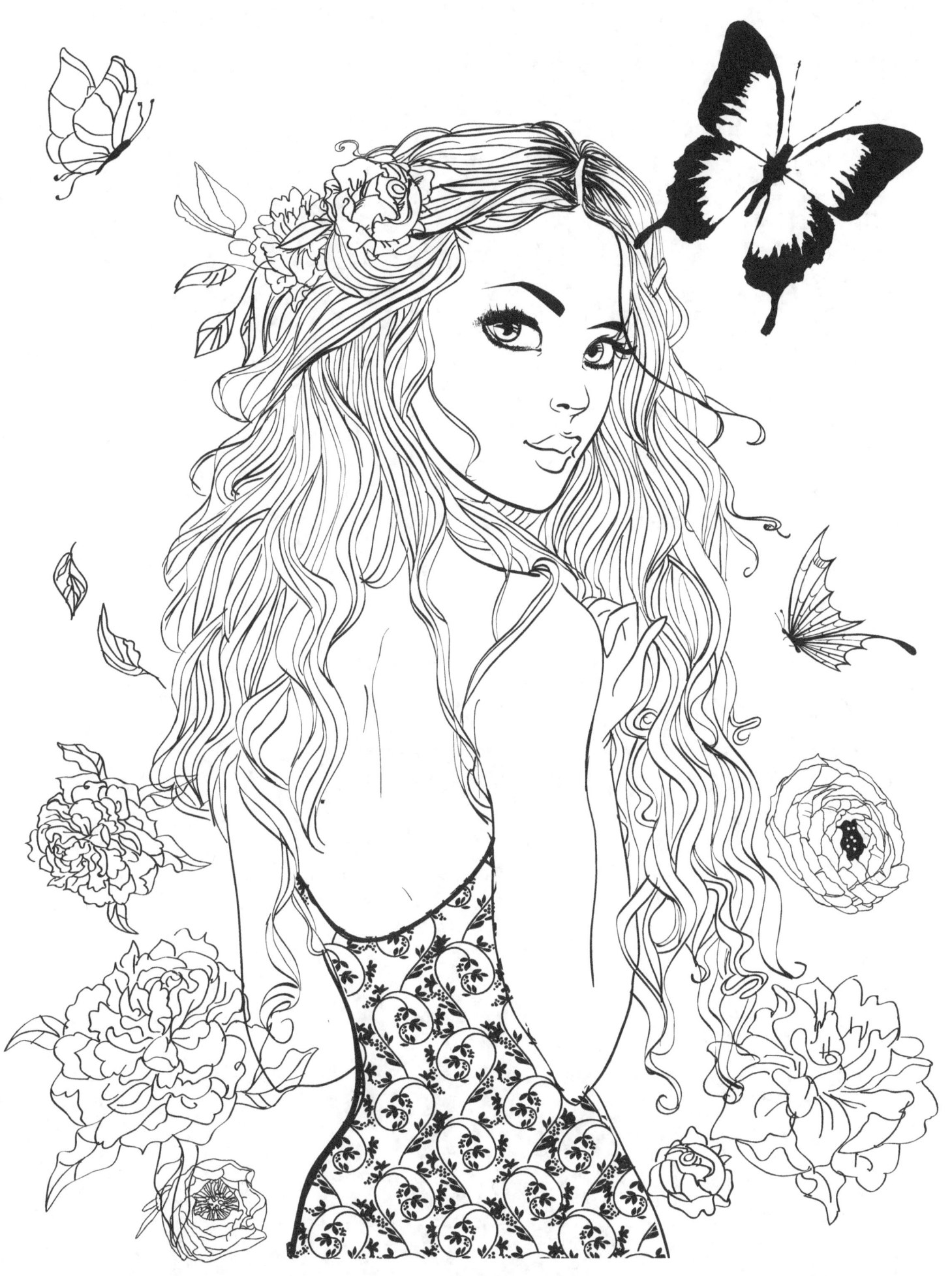

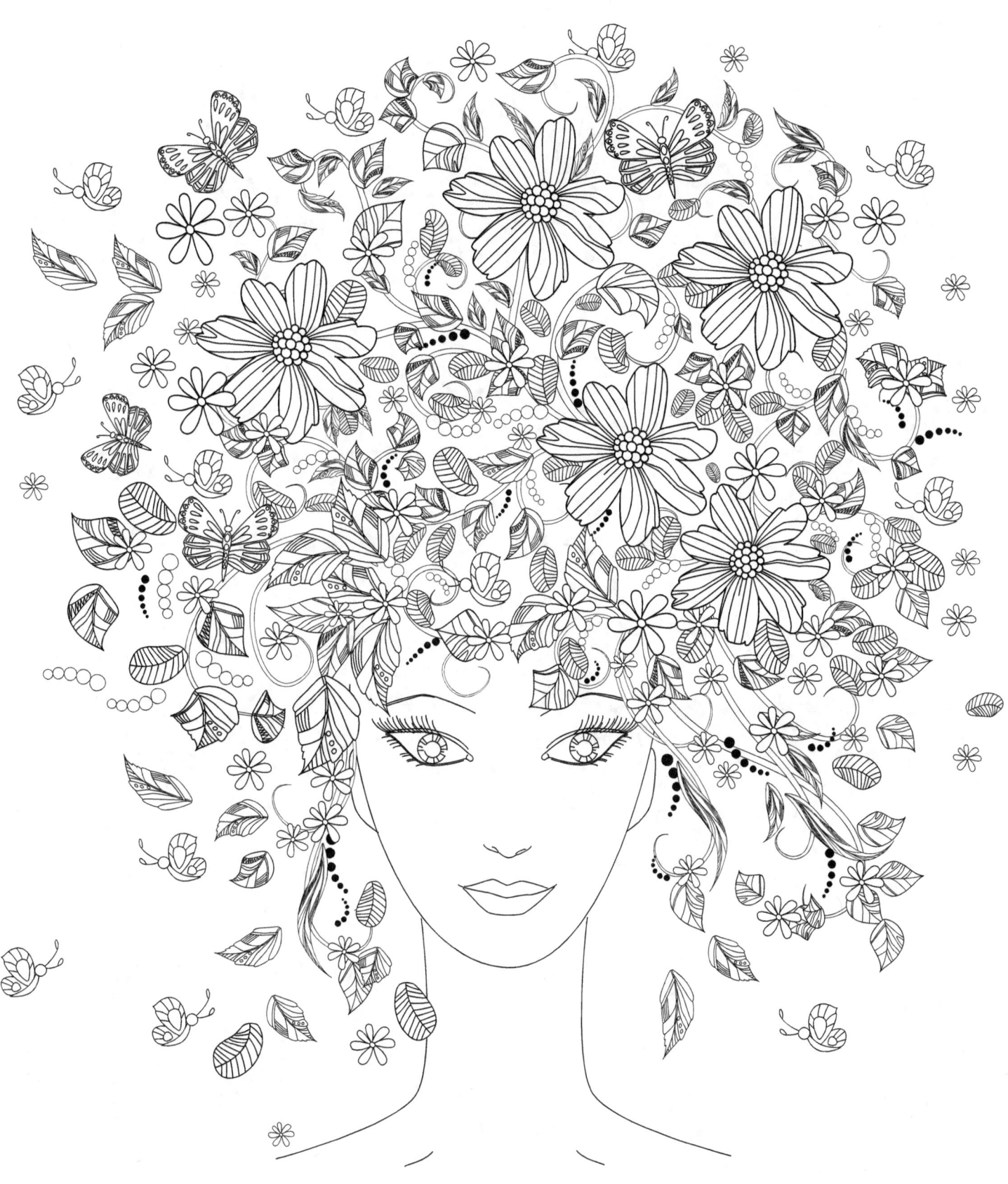

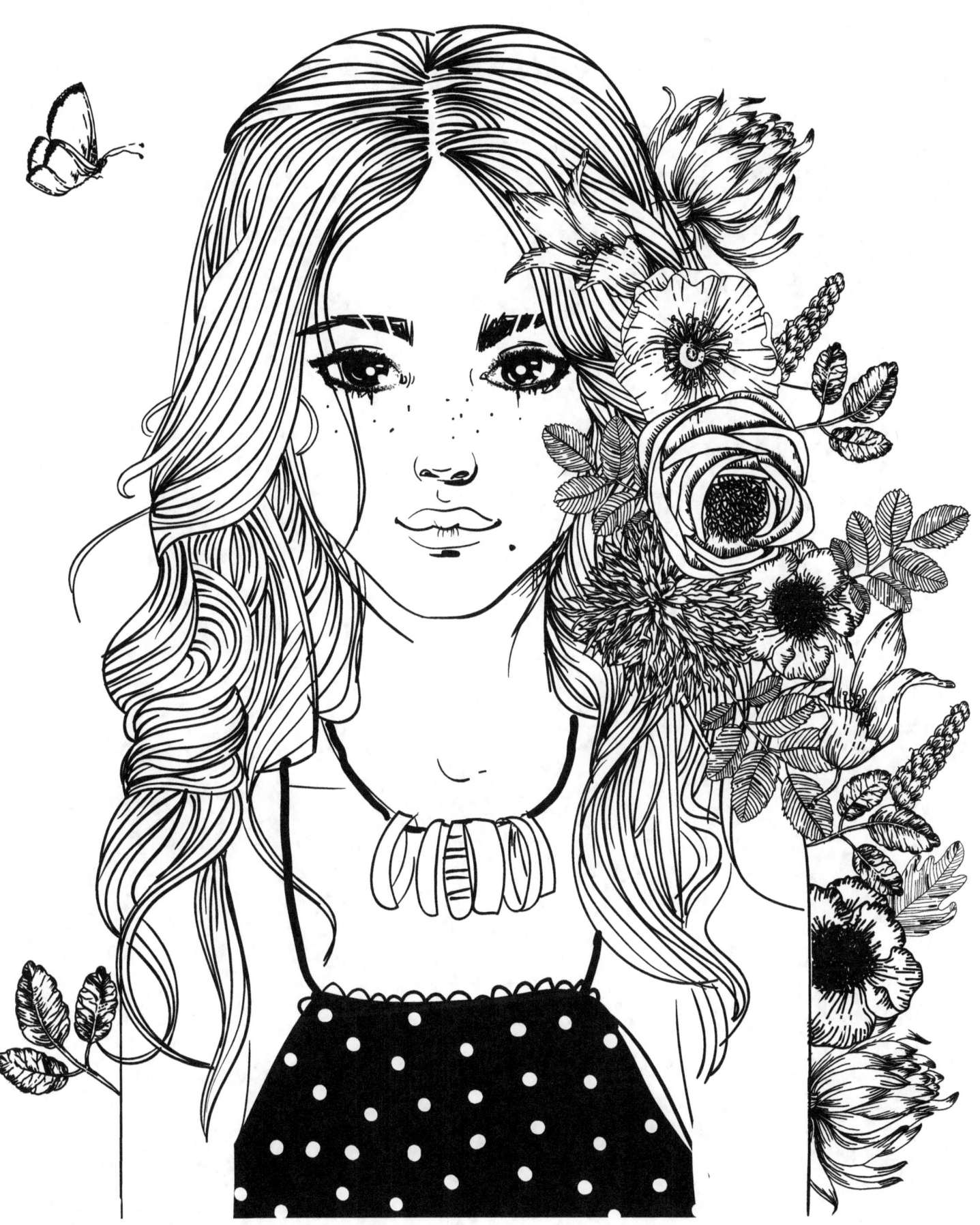

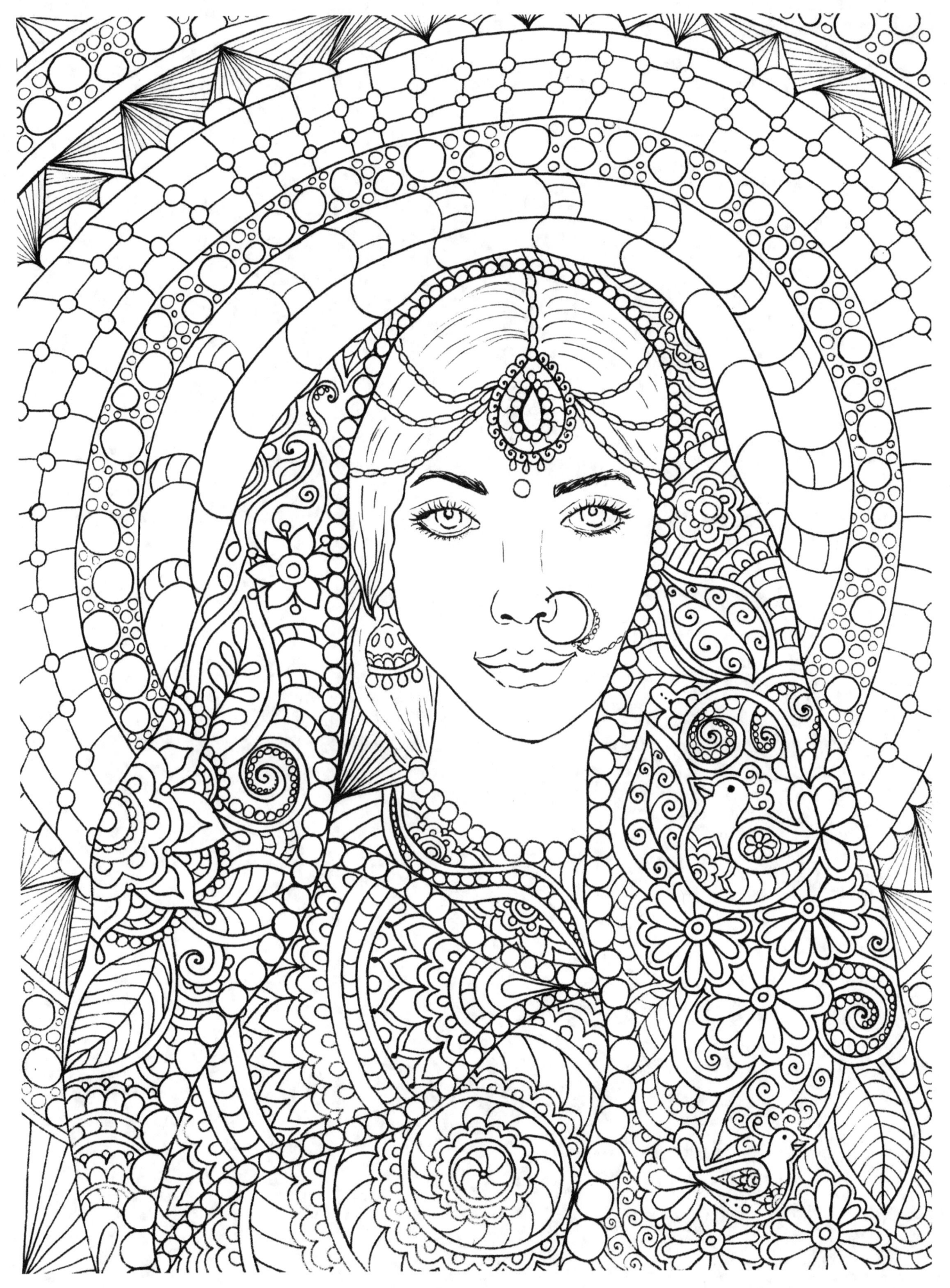

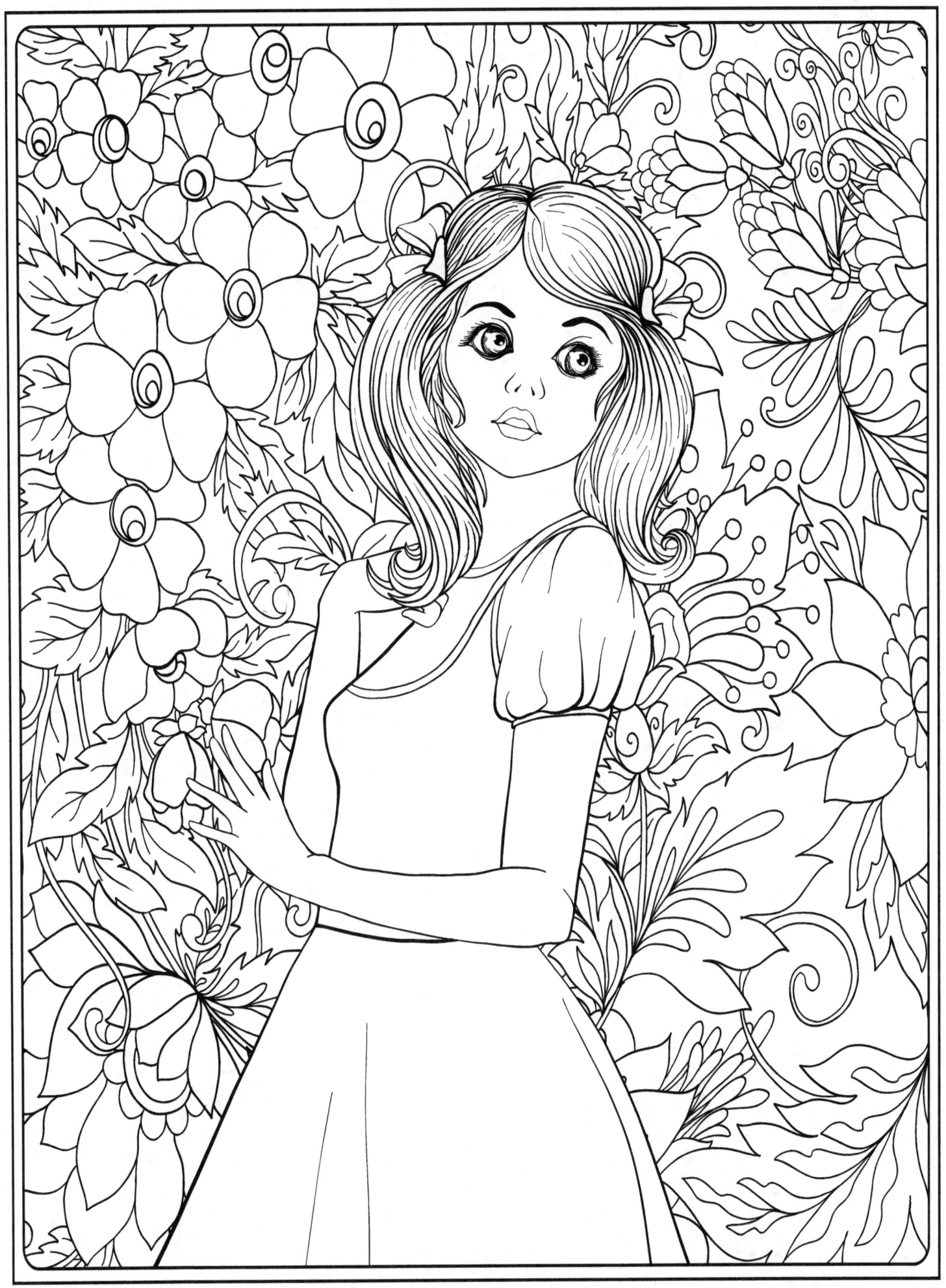

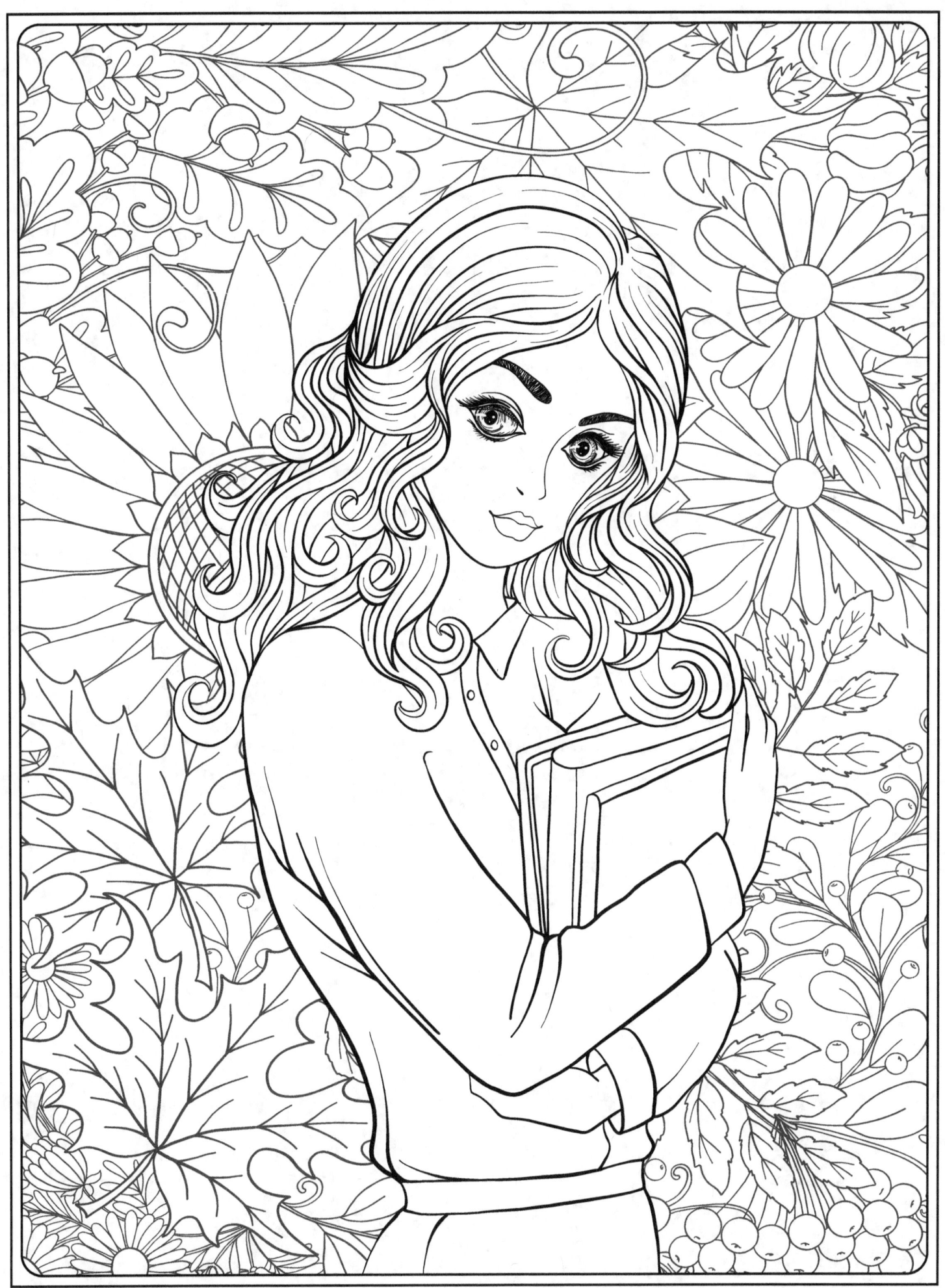

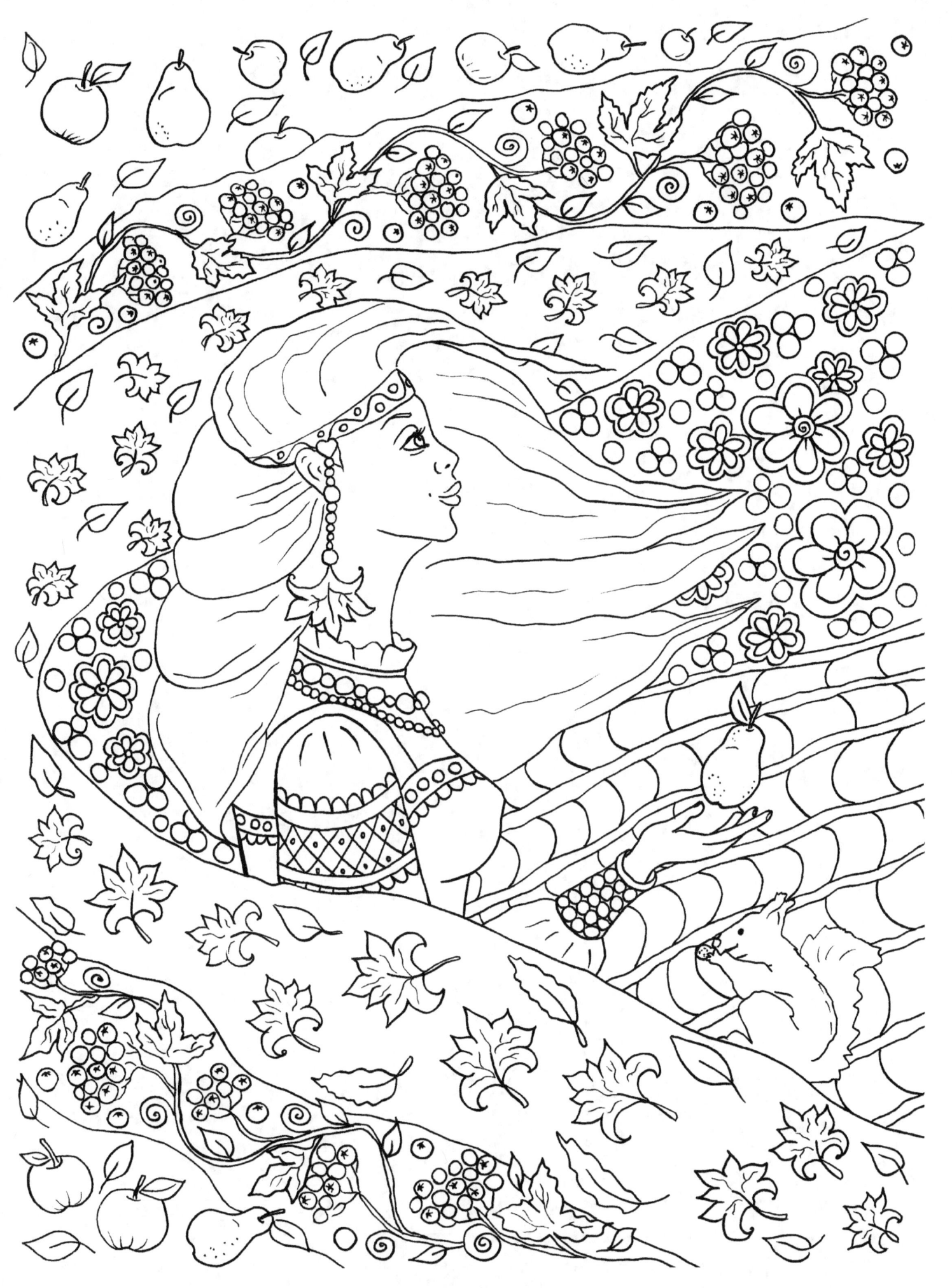

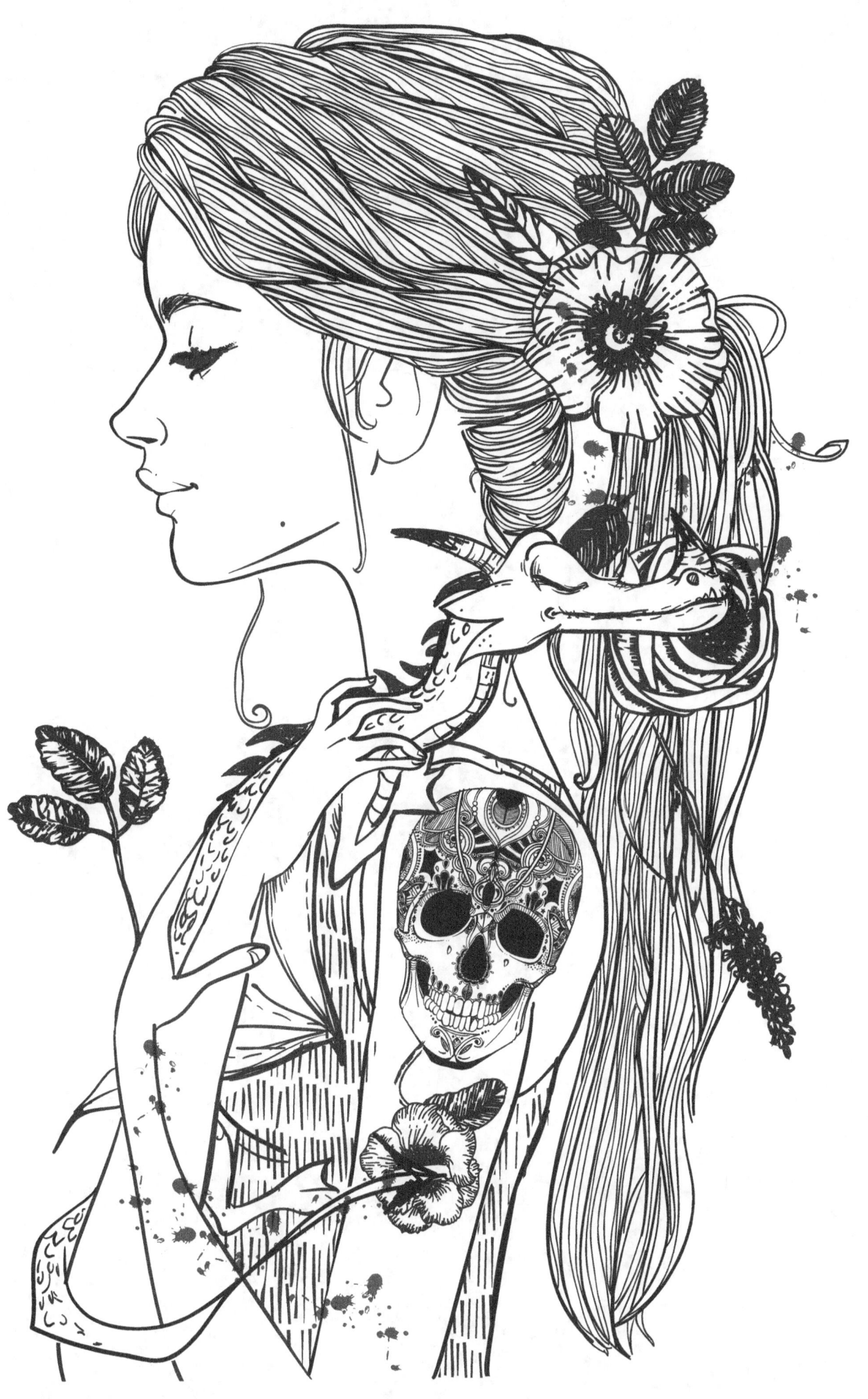

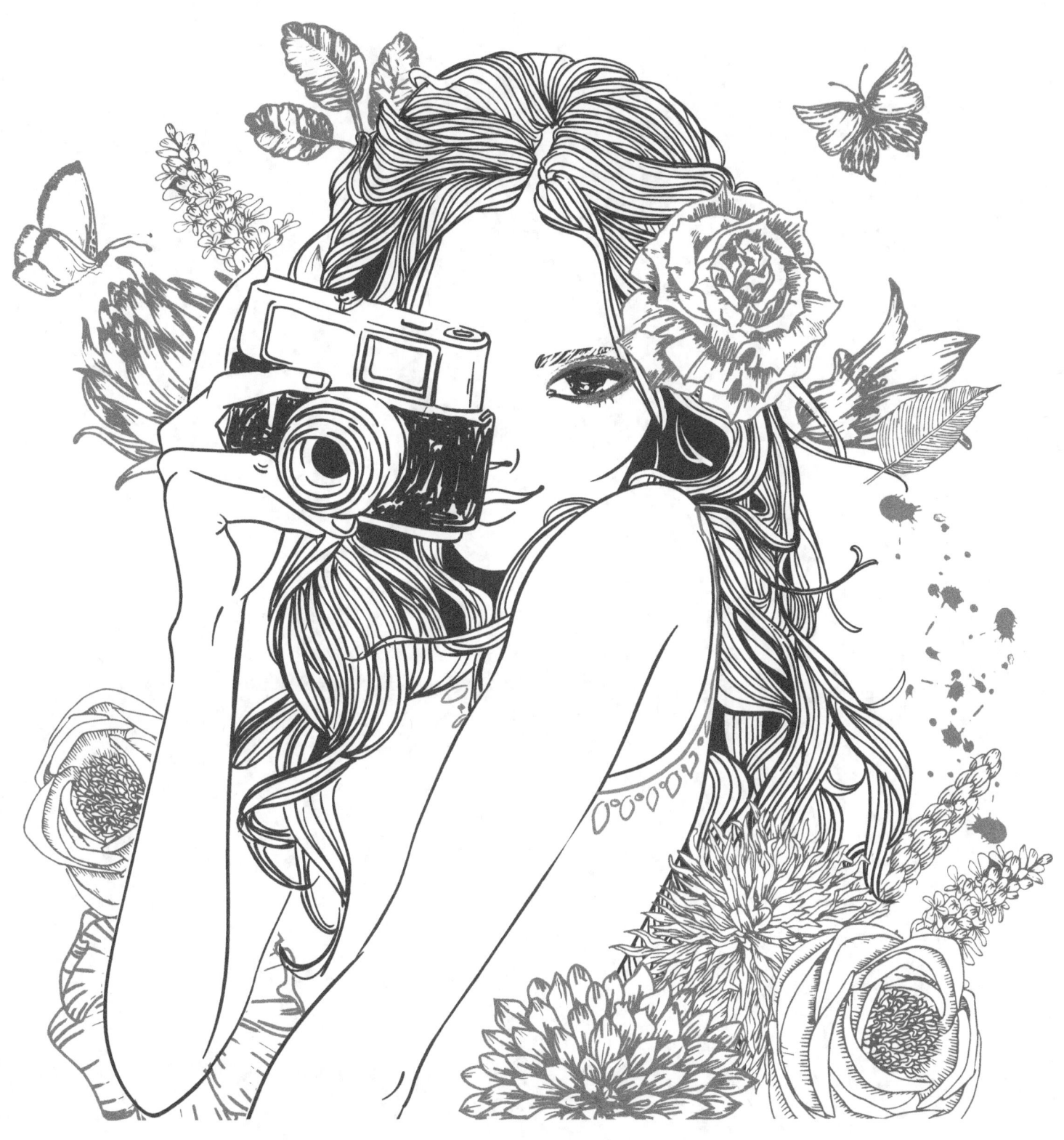

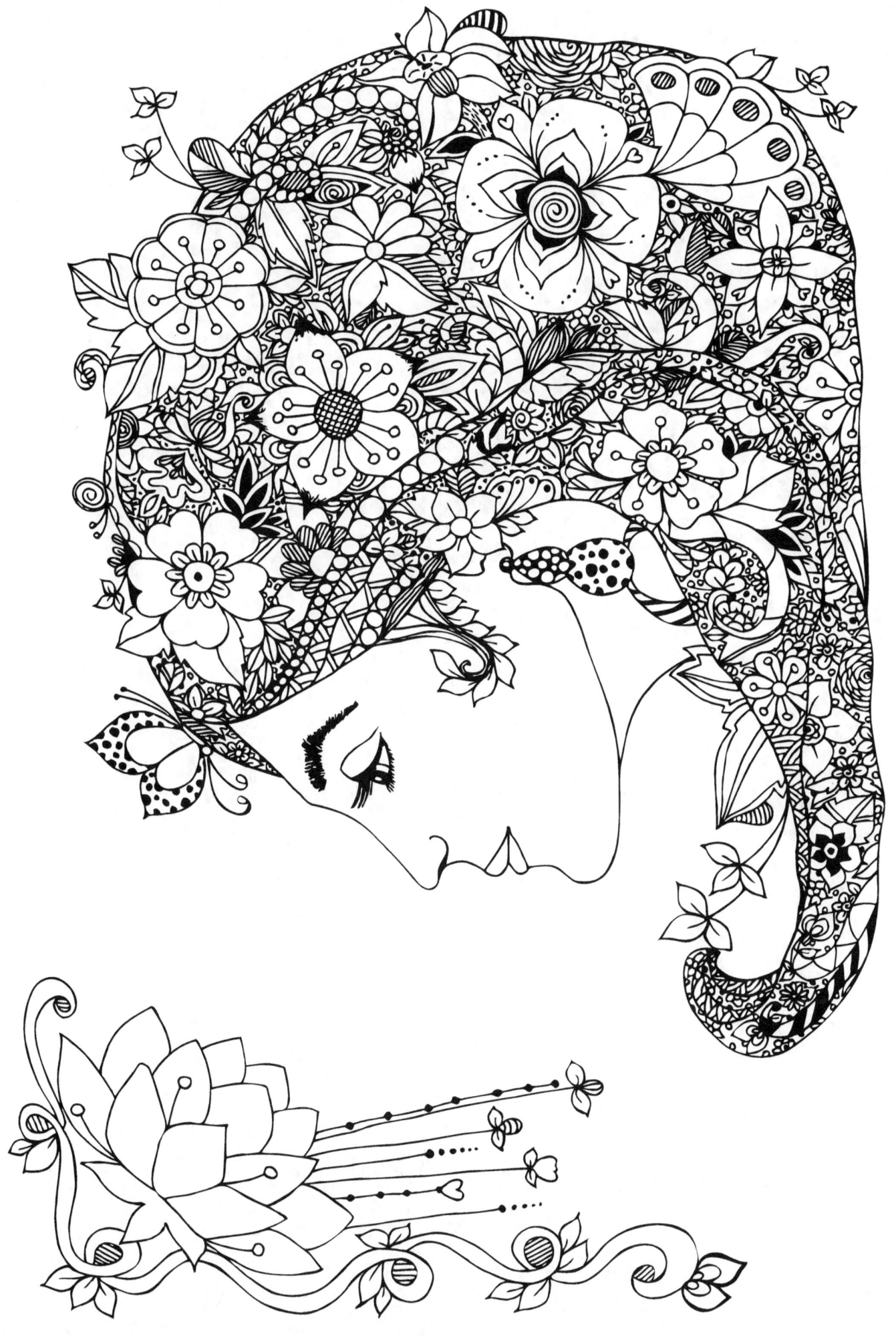

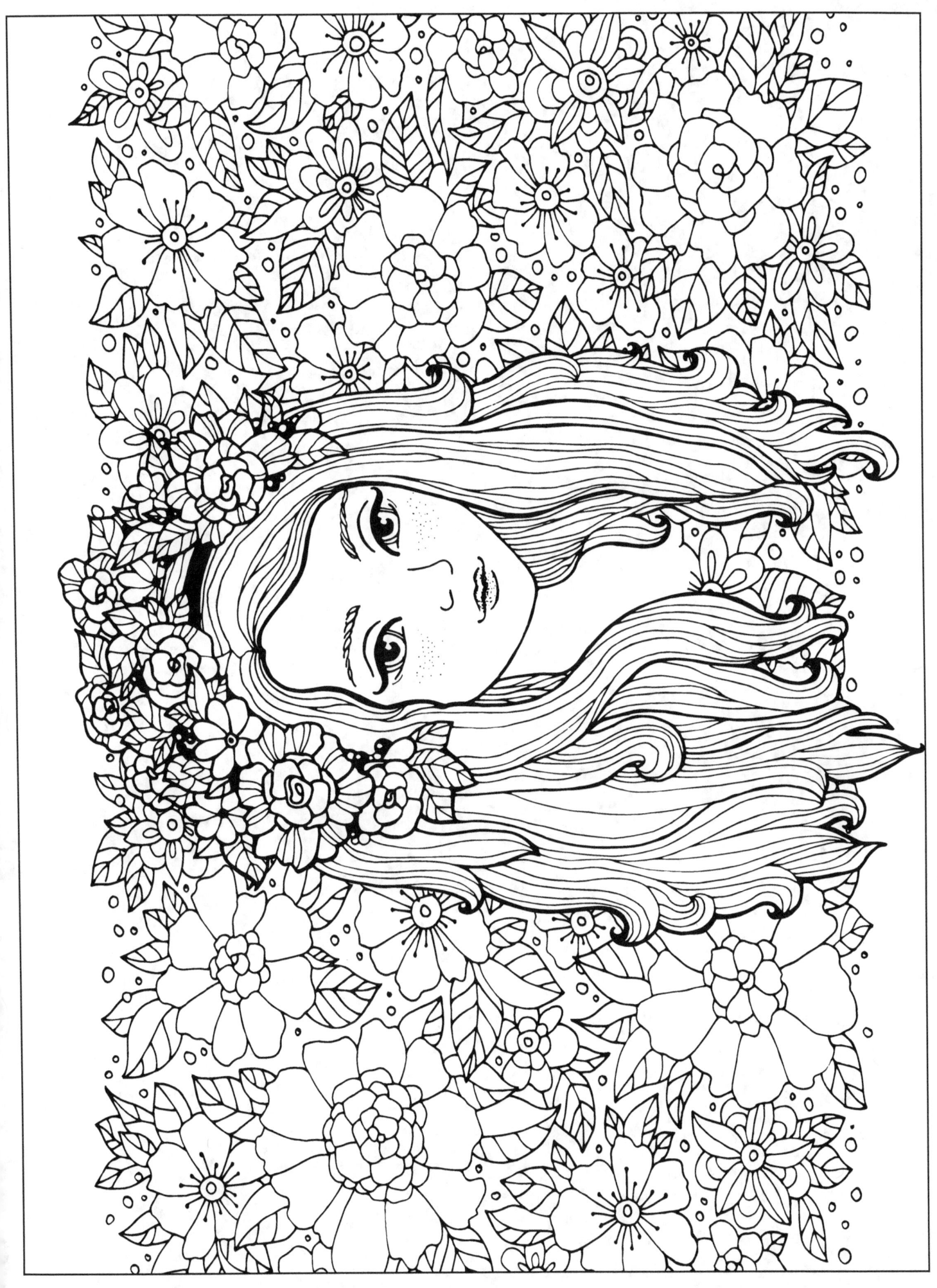

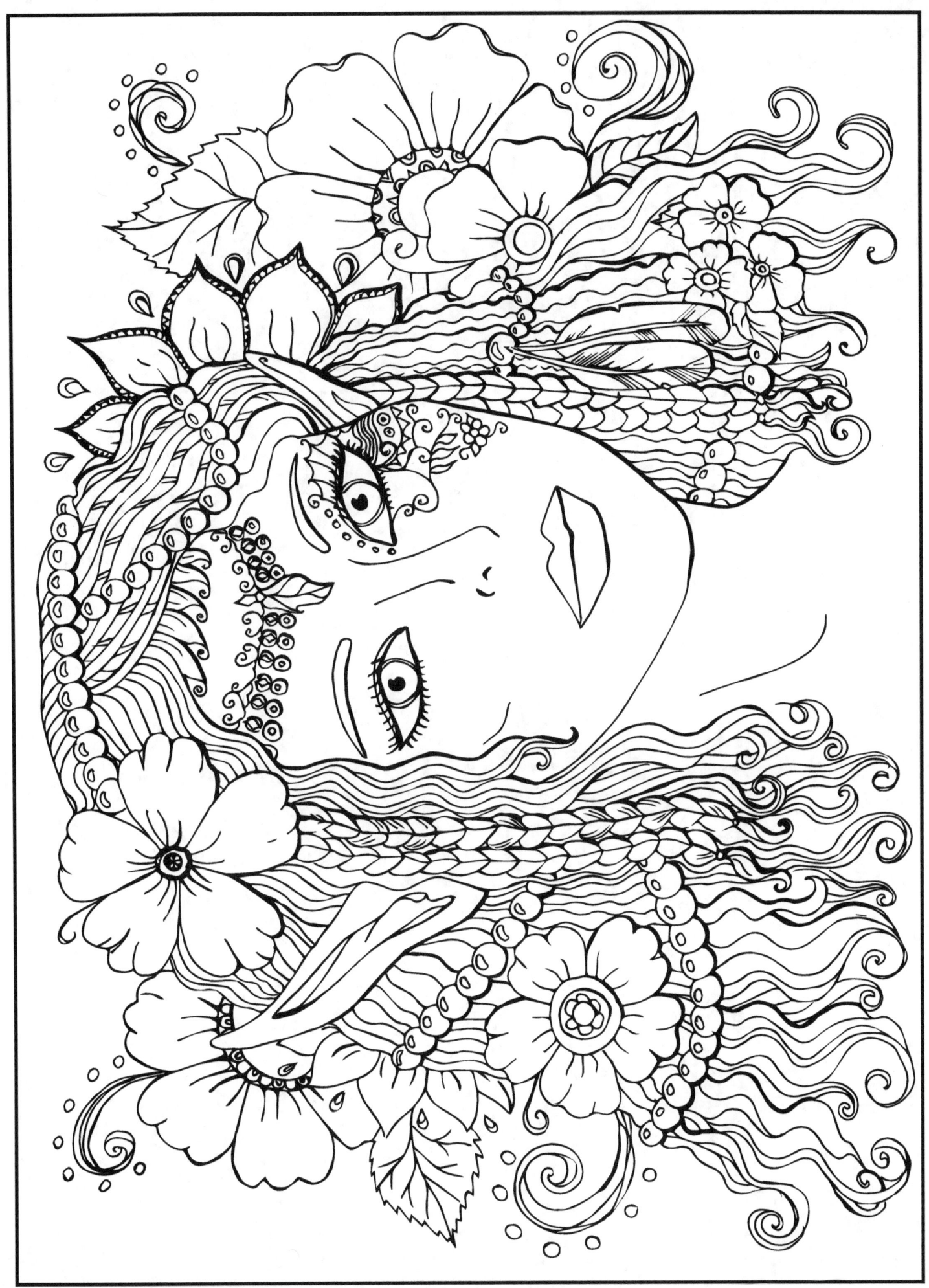

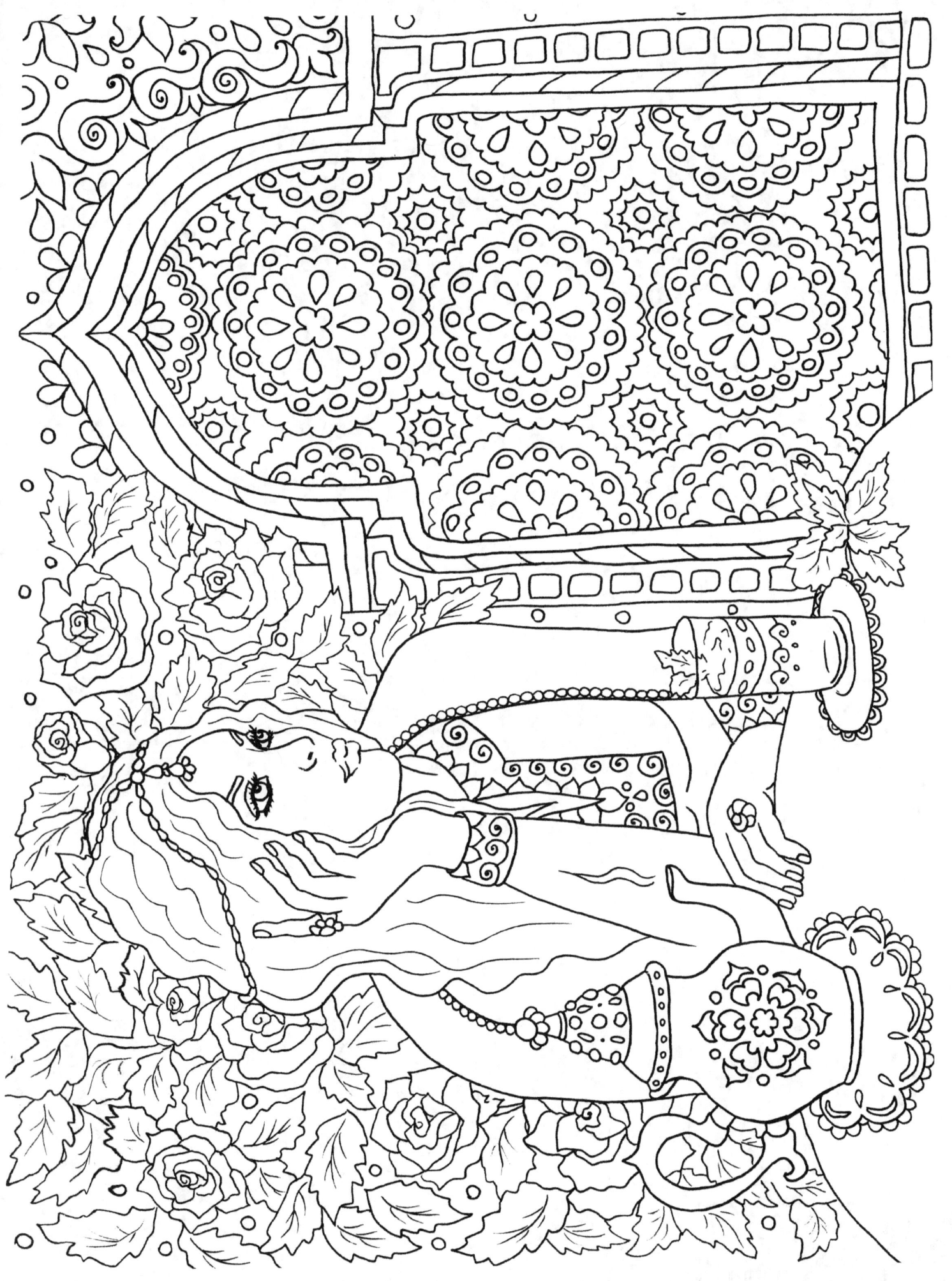